Great Recipes from San Francisco

Harvey Steiman

 J.P. Tarcher, Inc., Los Angeles

Great Recipes from San Francisco

FAVORITE DISHES OF THE CITY'S LEADING RESTAURANTS

To Kate,
my favorite dumpling

Design: Barbara Monahan
Illustration: Carol King

Art Direction: John Brogna

Manufactured in the United States of America

Published by J.P. Tarcher, Inc.
9110 Sunset Blvd., Los Angeles, Calif. 90069

10 9 8 7 6 5 4 3 2 1
First Edition

CONTENTS

INTRODUCTION

Since the Gold Rush, San Francisco has been known as a trencherman's paradise. The Forty-Niners who struck it rich knew they could spend some of their newfound wealth on a good meal in San Francisco—and get their money's worth. The reputation for serious eating has been as much a part of The City's lure as the Golden Gate Bridge and the cable cars. Tourists may go to New York for theater, to Boston for culture, to Miami for sun, and to Los Angeles to see movie stars, but they come to San Francisco to eat.

What makes San Francisco such a great town for eating out? Part of the answer lies in the quality of the ingredients available. A restaurant can only be as good as the food that comes in its back door, and the bounty of California's fertile farmland and the Pacific Ocean are at San Francisco's doorstep. The widest variety of produce in the country (the state produces more than 80 percent of the nation's strawberries, all of its artichokes, and more than half of its tree fruit), an excellent selection of regional seafood (Dungeness crab, salmon, halibut, Petrale sole, and Pacific red snapper), an abundance of locally bred delicious poultry (San Francisco restaurants serve a seemingly disproportionate quantity of chicken, duck, and squab), and, of course, Caliornia wines, all rank with the finest raw materials available anywhere.

A couple of other factors contribute to the deserved celebrity of San Francisco restaurants. The City's cooks have happily adopted and adapted the gastronomic contributions of all the cultures that have settled here —Italian, Russian, Mexican, Chinese, French, and recently Vietnamese—often with two or more cultures incorporated into the same menu. And the compact geography of The City, situated at the tip of a long peninsula, has concentrated thousands of restaurants on a relatively small piece of real estate, creating tough competition—and consequently greater effort on the part of San Francisco chefs and restaurateurs.

By extension, too, these factors apply to the entire Bay Area. Represented in this book are restaurants from as far north as the Napa Valley, as far east as Vacaville, and as far south as Monterey, all of which area San Franciscans think of pretty much as their backyards. (Although this is not intended as a guide-book for selecting restaurants, a roster at the end of the book briefly describes each and lists the recipes it has contributed.)

In selecting the recipes for *Great Recipes from San Francisco*, I wanted a sampling of creative dishes that reflected the personalities of the leading restaurants (though not necessarily the most expensive) and that were popular items on their menus. And I wanted recipes that could be done in an ordinary home kitchen, generally without exotic ingredients or extraordinary skill. Not all restaurant recipes, it should be pointed out, translate well to the home kitchen. A chef makes his sauce bases, cuts up vegetables, and prepares his garnishes hours before the restaurant opens for business. With all this at his fingertips, a chef can whip up complicated dishes in a matter of minutes. At home, one of those dishes could take hours to make because of the preparation time involved. Fortunately, not all restaurant recipes fall into this category, and I have made a special effort to select those that do not. This book, then, is a collection of dishes that amply represent the imagination and love for food that are the hallmarks of San Francisco restaurants, but that don't need a restaurant kitchen or limitless amounts of time to produce.

You will find included a goodly number of recipes that can serve one or two. This presented no difficulty, since good restaurants generally make their best dishes to order. Although most of the recipes are designed to serve six, where appropriate I have put recipes in a per-serving basis. And in some cases, notably a few soups and cakes, the proportions are for 10 or 12 servings. Every recipe has also been home-tested to insure that the proportions and the procedures are correct.

With few exceptions, all the ingredients used to test these recipes came from supermarkets or meat, fish, and poultry stores. Special ingredients, for the few recipes that call for them, can be found in the gourmet sections of large supermarkets or, certainly, in ethnic food stores. And please note that recipes that call for Pacific Coast seafood can easily be adapted to whatever is available fresh in your area: try blue crab for Dungeness crab, any flatfish for Petrale sole, grouper for Pacific red snapper. In addition, "prawns" in a recipe simply means large shrimp, and bay shrimp are the tiny shrimp. Finally, I encourage you to use the best ingredients you can find if you wish to duplicate the quality of these dishes. Good chefs insist on it.

These recipes evoke the creative ideas of chefs and restaurateurs who have helped make San Francisco's gastronomic reputation. With them, you can capture the essence of San Francisco's cuisine at your table. In short, I offer you a taste of San Francisco.

A Word about Serving Suggestions and Wine Recommendations

Following all of the entrées and a few of the appetizers, soups, and desserts, you will find suggestions for other dishes and wines to serve with them. In some cases, the suggestions describe the way the restaurant itself serves the dish. In others, the thoughts are mine.

Either way, don't feel constrained; they are only suggestions. If you would rather serve carrots than zucchini, go right ahead.

The same is true of wine. The recommendations are based on my experience of having tasted the wine with the dish. This is not to say you might not like something else better. Please note that I have not recommended specific brands of wine, but in most cases I have zeroed in on a specific type, such as "a light, tart red wine," or "a rich Chardonnay." Also, except for dishes that come from a specific national cuisine, I have recommended California wines, since some of the finest vineyards in the world stretch in three directions from San Francisco, and for most of us there is no compulsion to look any farther to satisfy our palates. Foods of any given nationality, however, tend to taste best with the wines of the same country, so I have also recommended imported wines with appropriate dishes.

—Harvey Steiman

Appetizers

Baked Whole Garlic

CHEZ PANISSE

A *whole* head of garlic? For each person? Mon dieu! No one could stand to be near you for weeks after you eat it, you may well guess. Actually, during the long baking process, the garlic loses all of its pungency; the interior turns sweet and soft, like butter, and it can be spread on crusty French bread. The garlic also makes a special garnish for grilled meat and poultry, but Chez Panisse's creative chef, Alice Waters, developed it as a first course for one of her annual all-garlic dinners. For garlic lovers, it is a breathtaking dish.

For Each Serving:
  1 whole head of garlic
  Salt, pepper
  2 tablespoons olive oil

Carefully make an incision around the garlic at about the middle, just piercing the skin. The object is to lift off the outer skin, exposing the tops of the cloves. Put it in a baking dish. Lightly salt and pepper the garlic, and pour the olive oil over it.

Heat the oven to 200° F. Bake the garlic for 15 minutes uncovered, then cover the baking dish and continue baking 1 hour or longer, until the garlic is tender. Baste occasionally with the oil.

Serve the garlic whole and warm (it can be reheated easily), with plenty of fresh, crusty bread.

Coupe Madagascar

VICTOR'S, ST. FRANCIS HOTEL

Green peppercorns, the darling spice of the nouvelle cuisine crowd, may seem an odd seasoning for a fruit salad, but it works. The green berries give the dish just the right kind of zing. Another creation of Hans Lenz, the St. Francis Hotel's talented chef.

  1 medium-size ripe pineapple
  20 green peppercorns
  1 teaspoon chopped fresh mint
  ¼ cup Grand Marnier or orange-flavored brandy
  ¼ cup honey
  1 cup plain yogurt

1 papaya, peeled, seeded and cut into 12 slices
6 slices strawberry
Additional sprigs of mint

Peel, core and dice the pineapple. Crush the green peppercorns with a spoon and combine them with the chopped mint and half (2 tablespoons each) of the Grand Marnier and honey. Add the pineapple, toss the mixture well, and let it marinate in the refrigerator at least 3 hours.

Beat together the remaining Grand Marnier, honey, and yogurt to make a sauce.

Divide the marinated pineapple into 6 portions, putting them in attractive glasses or plates. Garnish each serving with 2 slices of papaya and 1 slice of strawberry. Top each with the sauce just before serving, and garnish it with a sprig or two of fresh mint.

Makes 6 servings.

Eggplant Caviar

RUSSIAN RENAISSANCE

There isn't a bit of caviar in it, but the coarse texture and the practice of spreading it on crackers or toasted croutons earned this appetizer its nickname. It will keep for weeks in the refrigerator, and it freezes well.

2 large eggplants, halved lengthwise
1 large yellow onion, finely chopped
1 green pepper, seeded and finely chopped
3 tablespoons oil
2 tablespoons tomato paste
Juice of ½ lemon
1 teaspoon sugar
Salt, pepper

Heat the oven to 325° F. Grease a baking pan large enough to hold the four eggplant halves. Place the eggplants face down and bake them for 30 minutes. Peel off the skin and finely chop the eggplants.

Meanwhile, sauté the onions and peppers in the oil until they are soft and slightly browned. Add the eggplant, tomato paste, lemon juice, and sugar. Fry the mixture for 10 minutes. Add salt and pepper to taste—oversalt slightly since the mixture will lose seasoning somewhat as it chills.

Refrigerate the mixture in a glass or ceramic container. Serve it chilled, garnished with black olives and parsley sprigs. Serve it with triangles of pita bread or crackers as a spread or a dip.

Makes 6 servings.

Nasu Dengaka

AKASAKA

Ground chicken is the base for this unusual and savory sauce. Miso is a soybean paste sold in many health food stores. Be sure to use tamari soy, not the regular Japanese soy sauce, which is much too salty. If you can't find tamari, cut the amount of soy sauce in half and make up the difference with water.

3 medium eggplants
3 chicken leg quarters, skinned and boned
Oil for deep-frying or or brushing the eggplants for baking
3 cups white miso (soybean paste)
½ cup light (tamari) soy sauce
½ cup sugar
½ cup sake (Japanese rice wine)

Cut the eggplants in half lengthwise. With a fork or a pointed chopstick, poke holes in the exposed flesh of the eggplants, but do not pierce the skin. This helps the eggplants cook faster. Grind the chicken or chop it finely. Heat 2 quarts of oil for deep-frying, or heat an oven to 375° F. for baking the eggplants.

Put the eggplants in a deep-fryer for 2 or 3 minutes, just until they are cooked through, or brush them lavishly with oil and cook them on a baking sheet in the oven, face down, for 30 minutes.

Heat 1 tablespoon of oil in a skillet, then add the chicken. Sauté the chicken until it turns white, then add the remaining ingredients. Simmer the sauce gently until all the ingredients heat through. Divide the sauce among the eggplant halves and serve it warm.

FOR 1 OR 2: This dish can easily be made with one eggplant to serve 2 by using these proportions: 1 chicken leg quarter, 1 cup white miso, and 3 tablespoons each tamari soy sauce, sugar, and sake.

NOTE: Akasaka deep-fries the eggplants for this dish, but baking them basted with oil produces a satisfactory alternative.

Gambas al Ajillo

EL GRECO

In Spain, at cocktail hour, light dry sherries are served with hors d'oeuvres called tapas. The tapas, such as these Gambas al Ajillo, are usually savory rascals to encourage liberal consumption of wine.

1½ pounds raw prawns (large shrimp)
Salt
⅓ cup olive oil
3 or 4 cloves garlic, thinly sliced lengthwise
Hot red pepper flakes

Peel, devein and lightly salt the prawns.

In a large skillet, heat the oil and garlic until the aromas start wafting from the pan, about 45 to 60 seconds. Add the prawns, sprinkle them with pepper flakes to taste, and cover the pan. Cook just until the prawns are pink and sizzling. Serve this dish with plenty of crusty bread to sop up the flavorful oil.

Makes 6 servings.

NOTE: Be judicious with the pepper. About ½ to 1 teaspoon is enough for most palates.

Dry-Fried Prawns in Shell

KAN'S

Fingers tend to get sticky and unprotected clothes are liable to become spattered as enthusiastic eaters dive into this succulent preparation of jumbo prawns. Serve finger bowls as the next course. The big prawns are horrendously expensive, which makes this dish a splurge, but smaller ones just are not the same.

1½ pounds raw, unshelled jumbo prawns (shrimp)
2 tablespoons oil
½ teaspoon salt
¼ cup scallions cut into ¼-inch lengths, white
   part only
1 teaspoon soy sauce
2 tablespoons chicken broth

Wash and drain the prawns.

Heat a wok over a high flame. Add the oil and salt, bring it to a sizzle, and add the prawns in one layer, placing them flat with long chopsticks or tongs. Fry the prawns, turning them once, until the shells are brown and slightly charred.

Add the scallions, soy sauce, and chicken broth. Stir-fry the mixture quickly until the liquid reduces to a tablespoon or so, about 1 minute. Serve it immediately.

Makes 6 servings.

Marinated Squid

ALIOTO'S

Friends who otherwise recoil from the idea of eating squid have found themselves consuming this dish with gusto after the first tentative taste. If your guests are squeamish, save the tentacles.

The Squid:
2 pounds squid, cleaned
¼ cup vinegar
Water
½ lemon, sliced
1 bay leaf
½ teaspoon baking soda (optional)

The Marinade:
1 cup oil
½ cup red wine vinegar
3 cloves garlic, crushed
1 teaspoon chopped parsley
Salt, pepper
Pinch of fresh oregano

Rinse the squid and cut it in half lengthwise.

In a large saucepan, combine the ¼ cup vinegar with enough water to cover the squid. Add the lemon and the bay leaf. Bring the mixture to a boil. Add the squid. Let the mixture boil until the squid turns solid white. Pinch the squid to see if it is tender. If it is, remove it from the liquid and drain it well. If it is not, add the baking soda to the water and stir the squid for a minute or so. The baking soda should help it tenderize. Drain the squid and cut it into thin strips.

Combine the marinade ingredients with the squid, tossing them in the mixture to make sure every piece is coated. Let them marinate for at least 2 hours, stirring every 30 minutes. Serve immediately or keep refrigerated.

Makes 6 servings.

Crab Vinaigrette

ALIOTO'S

An alternative to serving California's native crab with the usual drawn butter or mayonnaise is to drown it in a garlicky vinaigrette. Crack every section of the crab first to ensure that the meat is well moistened and flavored.

For 2 Servings:

1 cleaned and cracked cooked Dungeness crab
½ cup olive oil
¼ cup red wine vinegar
2 cloves garlic, crushed
1 teaspoon chopped parsley
Salt, pepper to taste
Pinch of oregano

Put the crab in a glass or ceramic bowl or dish. Mix together the remaining ingredients to make a vinaigrette dressing. Pour it over the crab. Let it marinate, refrigerated, stirring the mixture every 20 minutes, for at least 1 hour. Serve it immediately or keep it refrigerated.

Steamed Clams

AKASAKA

Japanese dried bonito lends a distinctive flavor to whatever it is added to. Some don't care for the flavor, so try a little of the broth it makes before you make this dish for more than 1 or 2.

The Japanese Fish Broth:
2 cups water
½ cup dried bonito
Cheesecloth

The Clams:
3 dozen cherrystone clams
2 cups sake (Japanese rice wine)
1 teaspoon soy sauce

Boil the 2 cups of water. Turn off the heat and add the bonito. Let it steep for 1 minute, then strain it through the cheesecloth into a large saucepan or soup pot. Add the clams, sake, and soy sauce and bring it to a boil. When the clams open, remove them from the pot and serve them in their shells with small bowls of the broth for dipping.

Makes 6 servings.

Oysters Victor

VICTOR'S, ST. FRANCIS HOTEL

A variation on the same theme as Oysters Rockefeller, Chef Hans Lenz's creation relies on mushrooms, shallots and walnuts for its substance. Once you have the oysters open, it's possible to make this dish from scratch in less than 10 minutes.

For Each Serving:
6 fresh oysters
2 to 3 medium mushrooms
2 tablespoons chopped walnuts
1 tablespoon chopped shallots
3 tablespoons melted butter
1½ teaspoons chopped parsley
Lemon wedges or slices for garnish

Open the oysters, rinse them in cold water and place them on the larger half shell. Discard the other shells. Heat the oven to 400° F.

Chop the mushrooms and combine them with the walnuts, shallots, butter, and parsley. Top each oyster with this mixture and bake them for 4 to 5 minutes, or until the walnut mixture browns lightly. Serve them immediately, garnished with lemon.

NOTE: The number of servings is limited only by the size pan you have available to hold them and your patience with opening oysters.

Veal Tonne

BLUE FOX

In Italy, it is called Vitello Tonnato. On the Blue Fox's French-inspired menu, it is listed as Veal Tonne, and the chef garnishes each individual portion with strips of pimiento and patterns of whole capers.

The Veal:
   1½ pounds veal round, trimmed of fat and sinew
   3 ribs celery, cut in 2-inch lengths
   1 medium onion, quartered
   1 medium carrot, cut in 2-inch lengths
   4 cloves
   ¼ cup vinegar
   3 quarts water

The Sauce:
   2 ribs celery
   1 small scallion
   1 teaspoon capers
   3 ounces (½ small can) white albacore tuna, drained
   4 anchovy fillets
   2 tablespoons lemon juice
   2 cups homemade mayonnaise
   Dash of Tabasco
   Salt to taste

Tie the veal in a fat bundle, wrapping it first in cheesecloth, then tying it with kitchen twine. Put it in a 5-quart saucepot with the remaining ingredients for the veal. Bring it to a simmer, then let it simmer, covered, for 90 minutes. Drain the veal well but leave it tied. Put it in a deep dish or in a small pan with a weight on top of it to press out moisture. Put it in the refrigerator and chill it until it is firm.

To make the sauce, put the celery, scallion, capers, tuna, and anchovies through the finest blade of a meat grinder, or purée them in a food processor. Mix them well with the remaining sauce ingredients, adjusting the salt to taste. (Don't add salt until you taste it; the anchovies can be quite salty.)

To serve the Veal Tonne, untie and unwrap the meat and cut it into thin slices. Arrange the slices on a platter, or divide them among six to eight salad plates. Cover the veal with the sauce and garnish it with additional capers.

Makes 6 to 8 servings.

WINE: Chenin Blanc or French Colombard.

Hunan Onion Cake

THE HUNAN

Chinese cookbooks would have you believe that it is necessary to make a special dough for these cakes, roll it out carefully, and spend a lot of time at it. Nonsense. The Hunan is renowned for its version of this dish, and it uses plain Mexican flour tortillas. "It's the same dough," explains Henry Chung, The Hunan's practical owner.

12 flour tortillas, 7 or 8 inches in diameter
6 tablespoons sesame oil
2 eggs, lightly beaten
Salt
1 cup finely chopped scallions, including tender
   green
4 to 6 cups oil

Set up an assembly line: a stack of tortillas, a bowl of sesame oil with a brush, a bowl of beaten egg, a salt shaker, and a bowl of scallions next to or surrounding a work area large enough to accommodate one of the tortillas.

Put the 4 to 6 cups oil in a heavy frying pan slightly bigger than one of the tortillas. Heat the oil over a moderate flame to about 350 to 365° F. It should be hot enough for a tortilla to brown in about 1 minute.

Place a tortilla flat on the work area. Brush it with sesame oil, then egg. Sprinkle it lightly with salt, and 2 to 3 tablespoons of the scallions. Align a second tortilla over the first one and press them firmly together.

Slide this onion cake into the hot oil. When it is brown on one side, use a pair of tongs or chopsticks to turn it over to brown the other side. Meanwhile, prepare the next onion cake. When the cake is browned on both sides, hold it vertically over the oil to drain, then place it on a cutting board. With a chef's knife or a large cleaver, cut it in sixths. Slide in the next onion cake.

Makes 12 servings.

NOTE: This may seem like a lot, but most dedicated eaters can easily polish off one whole onion cake.

Shrimp Bonnet (Har Gow)

ASIA GARDEN

These delicate morsels are a snap to prepare if you have a food processor to finely chop all the ingredients and make the pastry. The only tedious part is rolling out the circles of dough.

The Filling:
1 pound raw prawns (large shrimp), shelled
3 ounces bamboo shoots, julienne-cut
1 ounce sesame oil
1½ teaspoons salt
1½ tablespoons sugar
1 teaspoon light soy sauce

The Dough:
2½ cups pastry flour
1 to 1½ cups boiling water

Finely chop the prawns and combine them with the remaining filling ingredients in a mixing bowl. Set them aside.

Sift the flour into a bowl. Add enough water to make a soft dough. Knead the dough until it is smooth, about 5 minutes. Let it rest for a minute. Cut off small pieces of the dough and roll them between the hands into 1-inch balls. Roll them out or flatten them with the heel of the hand into 3-inch discs.

Spoon a tablespoon of the filling into the middle of the disc. Bring the edges together to form a pouch in the form of a bonnet. The filling should show through the top.

Steam the Har Gow 8 to 10 minutes. Serve them hot.

SERVING SUGGESTION: This is a typical dish served in dim sum restaurants, where it is one of many tea cakes and pastries that are eaten in assorted combinations with tea. It can also be served as an appetizer before any type of meal.

Mousse of Duck Liver

L'ÉTOILE

One notch closer to ethereal than a simple paté, little custard dishes of this mousse make elegant appetizers for a special dinner. L'Étoile serves it with a brown sauce enhanced with a shot of brandy and garnished with fresh, seedless grapes.

2 duck livers
2 eggs
1 cup heavy cream
1 teaspoon salt
Dash of pepper
Dash of nutmeg
1 tablespoon Armagnac or brandy
½ cup sauce of your choice—tomato sauce, truffle sauce, Béarnaise, brandy sauce

Heat the oven to 300° F.

Combine the livers, eggs, cream, salt, pepper, nutmeg, and brandy in a blender. Process it until it is smooth, then push it through a sieve. Cook about 1 teaspoon of the mixture in a small skillet in a bit of butter to check for seasoning, then divide it among 6 small custard dishes. Bake them for 30 minutes.

Serve the mousse warm with a tablespoon of sauce on top.

Makes 6 servings.

Oeufs Farcis Chimay

L'ORANGERIE

French cuisine takes your basic stuffed egg a step further, bathing it in a lovely sauce. In this case, it is sauce Mornay, rich with Swiss cheese. Mushrooms add flavor to the stuffing.

The Eggs:

6 hard-cooked eggs
⅓ pound mushrooms
2 tablespoons finely chopped onion
4 tablespoons butter

The Sauce:

1 cup medium-thin Bechamel (see note)
⅓ cup shredded Swiss cheese

Cut the eggs in half lengthwise. Put the yolks in a mixing bowl, taking care not to break the whites.

Chop the mushrooms very fine. This is easiest done in a food processor, but it can be done by hand with a little patience. Cook the mushrooms and the onions in the butter over moderate heat, stirring occasionally, until the mixture absorbs all the moisture in the pan. Mash this together with the egg yolks. Stuff the egg whites with it.

Arrange the stuffed eggs in an ovenproof baking dish or casserole. Combine the Bechamel with the cheese and pour it over the eggs. (The recipe may be prepared to this point up to a day in advance and kept, tightly covered, in the refrigerator. In fact, the day's storage seems to improve the flavor.)

Heat the oven to 350° F. Bake the eggs for 20 minutes. Serve them hot with croutons or toast to soak up the sauce.

Makes 6 servings.

NOTE: Make the Bechamel in these proportions—1 tablespoon flour, 1 tablespoon butter, 1 cup milk. It will be quite thin but the cheese will thicken it considerably.

Dolmas

DAVOOD'S

Raisins, apricots, and apples add fruit flavors and a touch of sweetness to this unusual filling for grape leaves.

1 pound ground lamb
¾ cup raisins
1 medium onion, finely chopped
3 tablespoons mint leaves
¾ cup apricots (fresh or canned), diced
1 large or 2 medium apples, peeled, cored, and diced
¼ cup lemon juice
2 tablespoons finely chopped garlic
¼ cup finely chopped parsley
2 tablespoons cinnamon
2 tablespoons chopped coriander (cilantro)
1½ teaspoons salt
½ teaspoon pepper
1 jar (1 pound) grape leaves

Combine all the ingredients except the grape leaves in a large bowl. Mix them well. Drain the grape leaves. Overlap two grape leaves slightly to make a sort of rectangular shape. Near the middle place 2 tablespoons of the filling and roll up the grape leaves, tucking in the sides, to make a neat cylindrical package. Continue with the remaining grape leaves, arranging the finished packages in a large baking pan.

Heat the oven to 350° F. Add a little water to the pan to keep the Dolmas from sticking, cover the pan with aluminum foil, and bake it for 40 minutes. Drain the Dolmas well and serve them with plain yogurt.

Makes 6 servings.

Su Mi

ASIA GARDEN

Supermarket produce departments in San Francisco sell "gyoza" wrappers, which are precisely the dough for this recipe, pre-cut in perfect 3-inch circles. Buying them saves time, but the dough is not difficult to make, and you can get a wonderful sense of accomplishment watching the pale yellow discs pile up.

The Filling:

¾ pound boneless pork
1 ounce dried black mushrooms, soaked in warm
　　water and squeezed dry
⅓ pound raw prawns (large shrimp), peeled
1 teaspoon sesame oil
1 teaspoon salt
3 tablespoons sugar
2 teaspoons light soy sauce
¼ cup fresh pork fat, finely chopped (optional)

The Dough:

2 cups pastry flour
2 whole eggs

Finely chop the pork, mushrooms, and prawns. Mix them with the sesame oil, salt, sugar, soy sauce, and pork fat. Set them aside.

Mix the flour and egg with your hands to form a dough. Knead it until it is smooth, about 5 minutes. Cut off small pieces to form 1-inch balls. Flatten or roll the balls into discs 3 inches wide.

Spoon 1 tablespoon of the filling into the center of each disc. Fold the outer edge of the noodle casing up but not quite over the filling to make a cylinder. The filling should be visible through the top. You're actually forming a small cup to hold the filling. The moistness of the filling should hold the dough in place.

Steam the Su Mi 8 to 10 minutes. Serve them hot.

Makes 6 servings.

SERVING SUGGESTION: This is another typical dim sum pastry, which can also be used as an appetizer for any kind of meal. As at the tea houses, serve this and other dim sum morsels with good Chinese tea, oolong or jasmine.

Soups

Gazpacho Andaluz

EL GRECO

Arguments will continue among aficionados on the proper way to prepare and serve this simple cold vegetable soup. Some insist the ingredients must be chopped by hand to retain texture. Others say no, the texture comes from the array of chopped vegetable garnishes, which are added to taste by the diner, and that the soup must be smooth. I am of the latter school of thought, and so is El Greco.

The Soup:
5 fresh, ripe tomatoes
¼ green pepper, seeded
3 cloves garlic, crushed
2 slices sourdough bread, soaked in water
¼ cup olive oil
2 tablespoons lemon juice
Salt, pepper to taste

The Garnish:
1 cup chopped cucumber
1 cup chopped onion
1 cup chopped green pepper
1 cup oven-dried (not fried) croutons

Put the tomatoes, pepper, garlic, bread, oil, and lemon juice in a blender. Purée it, then strain it through a sieve. Season it with salt and pepper. Chill the soup, and serve it with little cups of the garnishes.

Makes 6 servings.

Chilled Cucumber and Dill Soup

MACARTHUR PARK

Cucumbers and dill are a classic match, and this simple cold soup combines the flavors for a refreshing summer meal-starter.

6 medium cucumbers, peeled and seeded
1 medium onion, chopped
3 ribs celery, chopped

2 large potatoes, chopped
2 tablespoons fresh dill, chopped (or 1 tablespoon dried)
2 cups heavy cream
Salt, pepper
Few drops Tabasco

Chop 5 of the cucumbers and put them in a soup pot with the onion, celery, potatoes, and 2 quarts (8 cups) water. Bring them to a boil, reduce the heat, and let them simmer for 45 minutes. Let the mixture cool, then purée it in a blender or food processor.

Finely dice the remaining cucumber. Add it along with the dill and the cream to the soup. Season it to taste with salt, pepper, and Tabasco, oversalting it slightly. Chill the soup. Check the seasoning again before serving it; chilling tends to dull the saltiness.

Makes 6 servings.

Cream of Artichoke Soup with Crushed Hazelnuts

FOURNOU'S OVENS

Don't omit the crucial step of roasting the filberts, which brings out their flavor and lifts this soup into the rarefied atmosphere of the truly great original dishes of San Francisco. When they are in season and cheap, take the time to trim a few artichokes down to their bottoms, cook them, and keep them frozen. With the frozen artichoke bottoms on hand, the dish is a snap.

4 large artichokes
6 cups chicken broth
1¼ to 1½ ounces hazelnuts (filberts), shelled
¼ cup rice
Salt, pepper
¾ cup heavy cream
2 or 3 tablespoons dry sherry

Remove all the leaves and stems from the artichokes. Clean and scoop out the choke, leaving only the bottoms. Poach the artichokes for 1 hour in water. Drain them. Put the artichokes and the broth in a large saucepan.

Spread the hazelnuts on a baking sheet and roast them at 250° F. for 10 minutes, or until they are golden brown. Crush them in a food processor or nut grinder, and add them to the broth with the rice.

Simmer the broth for 30 minutes. Purée the soup and pass it through a sieve to remove any pieces of nut, or string from the artichokes. Bring the soup to a simmer in a clean pot. Salt and pepper it to taste, then add the heavy cream and sherry. Heat through and serve.

Makes 6 servings.

Mushroom-Clam Velouté

NARSAI'S

Bottled clam juice in no way diminishes the magnificence of this simple, elegant soup. The only difficult part is chopping the mushrooms, which is easy in a food processor. You can even wash the mushrooms instead of wiping them clean with a towel because they are going to be simmered in liquid anyway. The results are astonishingly good.

3 tablespoons butter
6 tablespoons flour
3 cups clam broth (or bottled clam juice)
2½ cups water
1 pound fresh mushrooms, finely chopped
1½ cups heavy cream
Salt, pepper

Melt the butter in a large saucepan. Add the flour. Stirring with a wire whisk, cook this roux over moderate heat until it turns a hazel brown color. Immediately add the clam broth, the water, and the mushrooms. Simmer for 5 minutes. Keep stirring until it is smooth. Add the cream and simmer for 5 minutes longer. Season to taste with salt and pepper.

Makes 12 servings.

Cream of Watercress Soup

COW HOLLOW INN

We are so accustomed to thinking of watercress as a salad ingredient or a garnish that we are inclined to forget that it has a fine, peppery, delicate flavor all its own. It is magnificent in a cream soup, especially when its flavor is pointed up with a hint of rosemary.

1 medium onion, chopped
4 tablespoons butter
2 medium potatoes, peeled and cubed
1½ bunches watercress, thoroughly rinsed
4 cups chicken broth or veal stock
2 teaspoons dry rosemary leaves
1 bay leaf
Pinch of nutmeg
Salt, pepper
1 cup half-and-half or sour cream

In a large saucepan, sauté the onion in the butter until it is soft. Add the potatoes and 1 bunch of watercress; stir it well, and add the broth. When the soup boils, add the rosemary, bay leaf, and nutmeg. Cover the pot, reduce the heat, and let it simmer for 1 hour. Remove the bay leaf.

Put the mixture through a food mill or purée it in a food processor. Strain it through a sieve or a chinois, and return it to a clean pot to heat through. Whisk in the cream or sour cream and season the soup to taste with salt and pepper. Finely chop some of the watercress from the remaining half bunch as a garnish.

Makes 6 servings.

Cream of Broccoli Soup

ROBERT

No flour sullies this soup. It gets its thickening from potatoes. If you prefer a slightly rough texture, don't strain the soup. Robert's likes to serve it smooth as silk.

1 large onion, sliced
2 medium potatoes (10 to 12 ounces), peeled and sliced
2 tablespoons butter

½ teaspoon salt
¼ teaspoon pepper
6 cups chicken broth
1½ pounds broccoli (1 small bunch), cut in 1-inch
   chunks
1 cup half-and-half

In a large saucepan or soup pot, put all the ingredients except the broccoli. Bring it to a boil and let it simmer until the potato is soft, about 15 minutes. Add the broccoli and cook it for 15 minutes longer, or until it is quite tender.

Purée the soup in a blender or a food processor, or put it through a food mill, then strain it through a sieve. Return it to a clean pan, heat it through and stir in the half-and-half. Heat it through but do not let it boil.

Makes 6 servings.

Pumpkin-Leek Soup

THE NUT TREE

The Nut Tree figured out a way to give pumpkin soup a fresh taste even in the spring. Banana squash is so close to pumpkin in flavor and texture that, when it is combined with canned pumpkin, the effect is close to all-fresh pumpkin (which is, after all, a squash).

½ pound fresh pumpkin or banana squash, diced
1 medium potato, diced
2 tablespoons butter
1 small onion, sliced
3 cups chicken broth
½ teaspoon granulated garlic
1 cup water
1 can (16 ounces) pumpkin purée (unsweetened)
1½ teaspoons chopped parsley
½ cup leeks, thinly sliced
1 cup heavy cream
Salt, pepper

In a large saucepan (at least 3½ quarts) stir the pumpkin and potato with the butter over moderate heat. When it starts to brown, add the onion and continue to cook, stirring, until the onion softens. Add the broth, garlic and water. Bring it to a boil, reduce the heat, and simmer it 35 minutes. Add the canned pumpkin, parsley, and leeks and simmer 20 minutes.

Purée the soup in a blender, food processor or food mill. Return it to a clean saucepan to heat through. Just before serving it, stir in the heavy cream. Season it with salt and pepper. Serve it hot.

Makes 6 servings.

Lemon Chicken Soup

MACARTHUR PARK

Greek avgolemono soup was obviously Chef David Yates' inspiration when he created this delicately tart cream soup. It gets its body from a roux instead of eggs, but it also contains tender cubes of chicken. For those who like their soup more lemony, simply press the juice from the lemon slice garnish to release the flavor.

1 chicken, about 2 pounds
4 cups water
1 large onion, quartered
2 carrots cut in 2-inch chunks
1 rib celery, cut in 2-inch chunks
3 bay leaves
1 teaspoon salt
6 tablespoons butter
8 tablespoons flour
Few grindings of pepper
Juice of 4 medium lemons
2 cups half-and-half
1 whole lemon
Chopped parsley

Put the chicken in a large saucepan with the water, onion, carrots, celery, bay leaves, and salt. Bring it to a boil, reduce the heat, and let it simmer for 45 minutes, covered.

When the chicken is done, melt the butter in a second saucepan and stir in the flour. Cook it gently over moderate heat, stirring constantly, until it forms a smooth paste and the raw-flour aroma dissipates, about 5 minutes. Into this roux strain the broth from the chicken. Set the chicken aside to cool and discard the vegetables. Bring the soup to a boil, reduce the heat and let it simmer 30 minutes.

When the chicken is cool enough to handle, remove the skin and discard it. Trim the meat from the carcass. Discard the bones and dice the meat into ¼-inch pieces. Season it with pepper.

A few minutes before serving the soup, add the diced chicken to the simmering base. Stir in the lemon juice and the half-and-half. Heat it through but do not let it boil. Cut the remaining lemon into thin slices. Serve the soup with a thin slice of lemon and a tiny sprinkling of chopped parsley floating on top of each bowl.

Makes 6 servings.

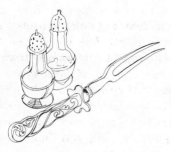

Winter Melon Soup

EMPRESS OF CHINA

The soup cooks inside a whole winter melon, which is fairly large, so this dish is best reserved for occasions when 10 or 12 hungry eaters are gathered around your table. As an alternative, you can always cut the skinned and seeded melon into ½-inch cubes and simply simmer them with the other ingredients, but it's not as spectacular a presentation.

1 winter melon, about 8 inches in diameter and 10
   inches long
⅓ cup diced bamboo shoots
⅓ cup small whole button mushrooms
⅓ cup lotus seeds (dried)
10 ounces white meat chicken (boneless), diced
⅓ cup dried black mushrooms, sliced
½ cup smoked ham, diced
3 to 4 quarts chicken broth
¾ cup thawed green peas
Salt to taste

You will need a utensil large enough to hold the whole melon and keep it covered while it steams. A turkey roaster is ideal. To prepare the melon, lay it on its side and cut it 3 inches from the top all the way around to form a lid. It is nice to do this in a zig-zag pattern to make it more attractive. Remove the "lid" and scoop out all the seeds and the pulp. Scrub the white powder from the outer skin.

When the melon is scrubbed clean outside and scraped clean inside, put the bamboo shoots, button mushrooms, lotus seeds, chicken, black mushrooms, and ham in the cavity. Fill it to within an inch of the top with chicken broth and replace the lid.

Set the melon on a rack in the turkey roaster. (You can improvise a rack with crisscrossed chopsticks if you have to.) Pour in about 1 inch of boiling water, cover the pan and steam the melon for 3 to 4 hours. You want to cook it until it is translucent and tender but still firm enough to stand on its own. It can steam on top of the stove or in the oven at 325° F.

When the melon is almost done, remove the lid and add the peas and enough additional boiling chicken broth to bring the liquid level back to within an inch of the top rim. Replace the lid and cover the steamer. Continue cooking for 10 to 15 minutes longer.

To serve the melon soup, scrape some of the flesh of the melon with the ladle as you scoop out the soup.

Makes 10 to 12 servings.

Hot Borscht

RUSSIAN RENAISSANCE

There is something soul-satisfying about a soup bowl brimming with the brilliant colors and hearty aromas of such vegetables as beets, cabbage, onion, and carrots. A blob of sour cream turning quietly pink as it floats in the center is a perfect touch.

2 pounds bone-in beef chuck, trimmed of fat
1 small head cabbage (about 1 pound)
2 carrots
4 beets
1 green pepper
3 ribs celery
1 large onion
3 bay leaves

6 peppercorns
1 small can (6 ounces) tomato paste
Sour cream, fresh dill

Wash the beef, then bring it to a boil in 3 quarts of water. When it first comes to a boil, reduce the heat to simmer and skim the scum that rises to the surface. Let it simmer 1½ to 2 hours.

Meanwhile, shred the cabbage, julienne-cut the carrots and the beets, and chop the pepper and the celery. Finely dice the onion and sauté it in a small amount of oil.

Remove the beef from the broth and reserve it. Season the broth to taste with salt and pepper. Add the cut-up vegetables, the onion, bay leaves, and peppercorns to the broth. Boil them gently for 30 minutes. After 15 minutes, add the tomato paste and stir it in well. Serve the soup with a dollop of sour cream and a sprinkle of dill.

Makes 6 servings.

NOTE: The reserved beef can be cubed and added to the soup just before serving to warm through, in which case it becomes a hearty main dish. Or the beef can be served separately as a main course with plenty of mustard and horseradish.

Burgundy Consommé with Escargots

CAFÉ MOZART

Where is it written that snails must be slathered with garlic butter and scooped out of their shells with tiny two-pronged forks? Or slathered with garlic butter and broiled in a mushroom cap? Nowhere, of course, as this soup proves convincingly. If you don't like escargots, try the soup without them. It's still delicious.

6 cups strong consommé
1½ teaspoons finely chopped garlic
2 cups dry red wine
2 dozen canned snails, cut in half
⅓ cup diced lean ham
Chopped parsley

Heat the consommé with the garlic and the red wine. Boil it until it reduces to 6 cups, about 10 minutes. (This need not be absolutely precise.) Just before serving, add the snails and ham. Heat them through for a minute. Ladle the soup into a tureen or into soup bowls and sprinkle with the parsley.

Makes 6 servings.

FOR 1 OR 2: For each serving use 1 cup consommé, ¼ teaspoon garlic, ⅓ cup red wine, 4 snails, and 1 table-spoon ham. After adding the wine, reduce the liquid to 1 cup per serving.

Harira

MAMOUNIA

A refreshing change from thick lentil soup, this has a light texture because it is to be drunk straight from cups at a Moroccan table, where eating utensils are forbidden. It makes a nice first course to serve in drink-ing cups in the living room before gathering guests around the dining room table.

½ cup chickpeas (garbanzos)
8 ounces lamb, diced
1 large onion, diced
2 bunches parsley, chopped
1 tablespoon fresh coriander (cilantro), chopped
½ teaspoon saffron
2½ teaspoons salt
1 teaspoon pepper
Pinch of ground ginger
Pinch of cumin
½ cup dried lentils
3 tablespoons butter
1 can (6 ounces) tomato paste
½ cup flour
Juice of 2 lemons

Put all the ingredients except the flour and lemon juice into an 8-quart soup pot. Add 3½ quarts of water. Simmer, stirring occasionally, for 1½ hours.

Add enough water to the flour to make a thin paste. Let it sit for a while to let the flour expand. When the soup has cooked for 1½ hours, stir in the flour paste.

Let the soup simmer for 5 minutes. Add the lemon juice and taste for seasoning.

To fully appreciate Harira, do not serve it too hot.

Makes 10 servings.

Fabada Asturiana

EL GRECO

Don't let the name intimidate you; it's just bean soup. But what a bean soup! The characteristic flavor comes from the sausage and seasonings. I find it a bit on the heavy side to serve as a first course. With a salad it makes a satisfying meal.

1 pound dry white beans
½ pound boneless pork, cubed
1 fresh ham hock
1 chorizo (Spanish sausage), or linguica, about ¼ pound, sliced
1 blood sausage (or Polish sausage), about ¼ pound, sliced
½ medium onion, finely chopped
3 cloves garlic, crushed
1 bay leaf
1 tablespoon paprika
1 teaspoon ground cumin
Dash of cayenne
Salt

Put the beans in a large pot. Add all the remaining ingredients except salt. Cover the ingredients with cold water. Bring the soup to a slow simmer and let it cook for 2 to 3 hours, or until the beans are tender.

Remove the ham hock and cut the meat into small pieces. Return the pieces to the soup. Add salt to taste. Serve the soup as a hearty first course, or add crusty bread and a salad to make it a peasant meal.

Makes 6 servings.

WINE: Any hearty red wine, from jug to well-aged Barolo.

San Francisco Crab Soup

VIENNA COFFEE HOUSE, MARK HOPKINS HOTEL

. A sort of crab chowder without the potatoes, this hearty soup gets its body from okra, like a gumbo. The Mark Hopkins' chef, Antoine Huber, has borrowed from New Orleans, French and Western cuisines for this aromatic and satisfying soup.

4 tablespoons butter
1 medium onion, chopped
1 medium green pepper, seeded and chopped
1 leek, white part only, chopped
8 cups (2 quarts) fish broth
½ cup rice
3 large tomatoes, peeled, seeded and chopped
1 teaspoon Worcestershire sauce
½ pound okra, cut lengthwise in thin strips
Salt, pepper
Meat of 2 large Dungeness crabs (2 cups, packed)

In a large saucepan, melt the butter and sauté the onion, green pepper, and leek gently until they are soft, about 10 minutes. Add the fish broth and rice. Let it boil for 20 minutes. Add the tomatoes, Worcestershire sauce, and the okra, and cook for 20 minutes longer. Season it to taste with salt and pepper.

A few minutes before serving the soup, add the crab meat. If the crab is already cooked, just heat it through gently for 1 or 2 minutes. If the crab is raw, simmer the soup gently until the crab is done, about 5 minutes.

Makes 8 to 10 servings.

Manhattan Chowder

SPENGER'S FISH GROTTO

Being a native-born Bostonian, I tend to frown on the practice of adding tomatoes to clam chowder. However, the soup known as Manhattan chowder has its devotees, and here is one of the better, more authentic recipes you will find for it.

4 pounds clams
4 slices bacon, finely diced
1 large onion, diced
2 tablespoons finely chopped celery
1 green pepper, seeded and chopped
4 ripe medium tomatoes, peeled and chopped
2 large boiling potatoes, peeled and diced
Pinch of thyme and parsley
2 tablespoons butter
3 tablespoons flour
Salt, pepper

Clean the clams and place them in a large saucepan or a small soup pot. Add enough boiling water to just about cover the clams. Simmer them until the clam shells open, about 5 minutes. Remove the pan from the heat. Remove the clams from their shells, letting the juice run into the pot. Discard the shells and any clams that don't open. Chop the clams and set them aside. Measure the clam liquid in the pot. You should have about 4 cups.

In a clean pot, brown the bacon gently to render its fat. Cook the onion, celery, pepper, and tomatoes in the bacon fat until the onions and celery are softened, about 5 minutes. Add the reserved clam juices, potatoes, thyme, and parsley. Cook the mixture 20 minutes, or until the potatoes are soft.

In a separate pan, melt the butter and stir in the flour to make a smooth roux. Cook it for 3 minutes, then stir it into the soup to thicken it. Add the reserved clams. Do not let the soup boil after you add the clams. Serve it immediately.

Makes 6 servings.

Dried Scallop Soup

EMPRESS OF CHINA

Dried scallops are horrendously expensive, but you only need a few of them to make this exceptionally flavorful special-occasion soup. The beauty of it is that it goes together in a matter of a minutes and it's easy. If the price of scallops is too awesome to contemplate, this soup can be made with dried oysters.

½ cup (4 to 6) dried scallops
1 cup white meat chicken (boneless), cut into thin
   matchsticks
2½ cups chicken broth
1 teaspoon salt (or to taste)
Dash of pepper
2 tablespoons cornstarch
2 tablespoons water
1 egg, lightly beaten

Soak the scallops in warm water for 20 minutes, or until they soften. Drain and chop them roughly.

In a wok or medium-size saucepan, combine the scallops, chicken, and broth. Bring them to a boil, add the salt and pepper, and let the soup boil for 1 minute. Dissolve the cornstarch in the water and stir it into the soup. When it thickens slightly, turn off the heat and gently stir in the beaten egg. Serve it immediately.

Makes 6 servings.

Fish & Seafood

Fisherman's Prawns

GOLDEN EAGLE

As simple as this dish is to prepare, it works on an astonishing number of levels. There's the intermingling of the marinade flavors, the sharpness of the horseradish against the bittersweet character of the marmalade. The prawns char slightly in the broiler, adding a smoky note to their naturally sweet taste and supple texture. Bits of the orange from the marmalade char with the shrimp, adding a special fragrance and texture.

2½ pounds large prawns (large shrimp)
½ cup olive oil
1 tablespoon salt
1 tablespoon leaf oregano
1 clove garlic, finely chopped
⅓ cup horseradish, grated
¾ cup dry white wine
2 tablespoons lemon juice
½ cup orange marmalade

Peel, clean, devein, and butterfly the prawns, leaving the tails on. Combine the remaining ingredients in a glass, ceramic or stainless steel bowl, stirring with a wire whisk to make a fairly smooth mixture. Marinate the prawns in the mixture for at least 2 hours, refrigerated.

Heat the broiler. Cover the bottom of a large casserole with a few spoonfuls of the marinade. Arrange the prawns on the marinade in one layer. Broil them for 3 to 4 minutes, at high heat, just until they brown lightly. Serve them with buttered rice.

Makes 6 servings.

SERVING SUGGESTION: Precede or follow the prawns with vegetable salad, such as Artichaut Châtelaine (see Index).

WINE: Because the dish is so flavorful, pair it with a simple, straightforward white wine, perhaps a Sylvaner or Chenin Blanc.

Gamberi alla Livornese

BLUE FOX

A simple pan sauce of white wine, lemon juice, and butter is just the thing to bring up the delicate flavor of sautéed prawns. Unless you have a restaurant stove or an oversized pan, better do the prawns in shifts if you plan to make more than 2 or 3 servings. The sauce can be made in the pan after both shifts are sautéed.

2 pounds large prawns (large shrimp), peeled and
   deveined
Milk
Seasoned flour
¼ cup oil
1½ cups dry white wine
3 tablespoons lemon juice, freshly squeezed
Salt, Tabasco
1 teaspoon arrowroot
6 tablespoons soft butter
2 tablespoons chopped fresh parsley

Split the prawns nearly in half lengthwise to butterfly them. Soak them in milk for 15 minutes, then drain them well. Just before proceeding to the next step, dredge them in flour seasoned with salt and pepper. Heat the oil in a large skillet. Brown the prawns quickly in the hot oil. Drain the prawns on absorbent paper. Pour off the oil.

Reserve a tablespoon of the wine and pour the rest into the skillet with the lemon juice. Bring the liquid to a boil. Let it boil for a minute or so to evaporate the alcohol, then season it to taste with salt and a few drops of Tabasco. Dissolve the arrowroot in the remaining wine and stir it into the sauce. When it thickens slightly, remove it from the heat and swirl in the butter, beating with a wire whisk until the sauce is smooth.

Return the prawns to the pan just to coat them with the sauce. Serve the prawns in the sauce sprinkled with the chopped parsley.

Makes 6 servings.

SERVING SUGGESTION: At the Blue Fox, warm garlic bread made of small sourdough rolls is served to sop up the sauce.

WINE: Any light, dry white wine, preferably the same one used to deglaze the pan. An off-dry French Colombard or Chenin Blanc adds a fruity sweet-and-sour aspect that we find pleasant.

Hot, Spicy Scallops

WHALING STATION INN

You'll need a large skillet to accommodate this hybrid of French and Oriental ideas. It starts off like a classic French sauté, then segues neatly into a variation on Chinese stir-frying. Needless to say, a wok works well. The flavors are bright and sprightly.

2 pounds fresh scallops
6 tablespoons butter
2 tablespoons vegetable oil
3 cloves garlic, finely chopped
1 large onion, diced
⅓ of a bell pepper, thinly sliced
1 quarter-size slice fresh ginger, crushed
¼ cup medium dry sherry
1 tablespoon Oriental fish sauce
Pinch of ground red pepper (or more, to taste)
1 teaspoon cornstarch dissolved in 1 teaspoon water
Salt, pepper

If the scallops are large, cut them in half. In a large skillet, heat the butter and oil. In it, sauté the garlic, onion, green pepper, and ginger until the onion softens. Add the sherry and the fish sauce. When the mixture boils, add the scallops and the red pepper. Reduce the heat and cook the scallops gently until they become opaque. As soon as they are done, stir the cornstarch into the sauce, turn up the heat briefly and taste the sauce for salt and pepper. Serve the scallops with the sauce over rice.

Makes 6 servings.

SERVING SUGGESTION: Broccoli or snow peas cooked quickly so they are still crisp perform in counterpoint to the smooth scallops and sauce.

WINE: Perfect for a slightly off-dry Gewurztraminer.

NOTE: Fish sauce is a soy-based, fish flavored condiment sold in Oriental stores and in some supermarkets.

Mussels "Poulette"

L'ÉTOILE

Essentially a thickened version of mussels "marinière" (seafood prepared with white wine), the velvety quality of the sauce makes this a special preparation for mussels. It's a mess to eat, but an unabashed joy for seafood lovers.

8 pounds fresh mussels
6 shallots, finely chopped
3 cloves garlic, finely chopped
3 tablespoons chopped celery
3 tablespoons chopped parsley
1½ cups dry white wine
Pinch of pepper
4 egg yolks
6 tablespoons unsalted butter

Scrub the mussels smooth. Take special care to trim the edge where the stem is that connected the mussels to the rocks. Pull the stem out to remove the entire piece, including the part that is hidden inside the shell. Wash the mussels several times in clear water until they become shiny black.

In a large saucepan combine the shallots, garlic, celery, parsley, and wine. Add the mussels and the pepper. No salt is necessary, since the mussels contain salty seawater. Bring the contents to a boil, cover and simmer for 10 minutes, or just until the shells open. Remove the mussels to serving bowls, draining all the liquid back into the pan.

To make the sauce, add the yolks to the pan liquids and beat them continuously over moderate heat until the sauce thickens slightly, but do not let it boil. Beat in the butter. As soon as it melts, pour the sauce over the mussels. Serve them hot.

Makes 6 servings.

SERVING SUGGESTION: Accompany this with plenty of crusty French bread for sopping up the sauce. With a salad, it makes a lovely late supper.

WINE: Muscadet or Macon Blanc has an affinity for mussels.

Fisherman's Stew

SCOTT'S

The next three recipes are of a family. They are all fish stews, but each has its own distinct character, achieved by the variation of only a few ingredients. Scott's serves the first, a riot of fresh fish and seafood, in individual iron saucepans. There is nothing fancy about it; it's just a seafood-lover's cornucopia.

1 carrot, diced
1 rib celery, diced
1 leek, finely chopped
1½ cups (6 ounces) fresh mushrooms, sliced
1½ pounds boneless fish, cut into chunks
2 dozen scallops
1 dozen prawns (large shrimp)
3 cloves garlic, finely chopped
6 cups fish stock (or bottled clam juice)
1½ cups dry white wine
1 dozen clams, opened
6 ounces cooked bay shrimp
6 ounces cooked crabmeat
¾ cup (1½ sticks) butter
¼ cup chopped parsley

In a large pot, combine the carrot, celery, leek, mushrooms, fish, scallops, prawns, garlic, fish stock, white wine, and clams. Bring it to a boil, reduce the heat and let it simmer for 8 minutes, or until the fish is just done.

Add the bay shrimp, crabmeat, and butter. When the butter melts, turn the stew into a large tureen (or serve it right in the cooking pot, if you prefer). Just before serving, sprinkle the surface with chopped parsley.

Makes 6 servings.

SERVING SUGGESTION: Lots of fresh, hot, crusty bread, especially sourdough. It needs nothing else.

WINE: A rich Chardonnay, Pinot Blanc, or White Burgundy.

Cacciucco Livornese

LITTLE JOE'S

In his restaurant guide, Arthur Bloomfield writes of this close relative to cioppino: "I have been moved to highly vocal exclamations from my counter seat by its virtuoso mingling of flavors." The secrets, patiently demonstrated to me by the restaurant's chef, are (a) a high quality broth of beef and chicken (not, as one might expect, fish), and (b) the rough texture of the homemade tomato sauce. Canned sauce will not do. The broth gets its seafood component from the clam liquor as the mollusks open their shells in the soup. This is definitely a one-dish meal. Each "serving" is really two or three normal soup bowls full.

For Each Serving:
2 tablespoons olive oil
6 medium prawns (shrimp)
⅓ pound rock cod or sea bass fillet
1 or 2 cloves garlic, finely chopped (optional)
Salt, pepper
3 clams
½ cup dry white wine
1 cup fresh tomato sauce (see recipe below)
1 cup beef and chicken broths, mixed
2 tablespoons chopped parsley

In a steep-sided skillet, heat the olive oil over a high flame. Sauté the prawns, turning them quickly, until their surfaces turn pink and they start to turn opaque. Quickly add the fish fillet, the garlic, a light sprinkling of salt and pepper, the clams, and the wine. When the wine comes to a boil, add the tomato sauce and the broth. Let the mixture boil until the clams open up, about 2 or 3 minutes. Sprinkle the surface with chopped parsley and serve it immediately.

To make this dish for more than 2 persons, a slightly different technique is more efficient. Use a skillet and a large saucepan or soup pot. Follow this procedure:

Sauté the prawns in the olive oil in the skillet, taking care not to crowd the pan. Do them in shifts if necessary. Put the prawns in the saucepan. Put the fish fillets and the clams in the saucepan, sprinkle them lightly with salt and pepper and a little garlic, if you like. Deglaze the skillet with the wine, scraping up any browned bits that may have adhered to the surface. Pour this into the saucepan. Add the tomato sauce and broth, bring the soup to a boil, and cook it until the clams open up, about 5 minutes.

The Tomato Sauce:
    1 onion, chopped
    3 or 4 cloves garlic, chopped
    ½ rib celery, chopped
    Salt, pepper
    ¼ cup olive oil
    1 can (3 pounds) Italian tomatoes, roughly
        chopped
    ¼ cup chopped parsley
    1 cup beef stock or 1 bouillon cube dissolved in 1
        cup water

In a 4- or 5-quart saucepan, sauté the onion, garlic, and celery in the olive oil, sprinkling them lightly with salt and pepper. Cook them until the onion and celery are soft. Add the tomatoes, the parsley, and the beef stock. Bring it to a boil, reduce the heat, and let it simmer for 1 hour.

Put the sauce through a grinder or push it through a coarse sieve. The idea is to retain a slightly rough texture, not to make it smooth like a canned tomato sauce. If you use a food processor, turn it on and off rapidly and stop when you reach the desired texture. Do not overprocess if you can help it.

NOTE: This sauce will keep in the refrigerator for about two weeks, up to a year in the freezer in an airtight container.

Cioppino

SCOTT'S

California's answer to Bouillabaisse is given a classic rendition by Scott's. The only deviation from the norm is the use of mushrooms, which add a welcome meaty touch. The recipe reads very much like Little Joe's Cacciucco Livornese, but the finished soup is a little more elegant perhaps.

For Each Serving:
- ¼ cup sliced mushrooms
- 4 ounces raw fish chunks
- 2 prawns (large shrimp)
- 4 to 6 scallops (small)
- ½ teaspoon finely chopped garlic
- ¼ cup fish broth or clam juice
- ¼ cup dry white wine
- 2 clams
- ½ cup marinara sauce
- 2 tablespoons cooked bay shrimp
- 2 tablespoons cooked crab meat
- 1 teaspoon chopped parsley

In an appropriate saucepan, combine the mushrooms, fish chunks, prawns, scallops, garlic, fish broth, wine, and clams. Bring it to a boil, reduce the heat and let it simmer for 5 minutes, or until the fish is just done and the clams open. Add the marinara sauce and heat it through. Add the bay shrimp and crab meat, and immediately pour the Cioppino into a large soup bowl. Sprinkle the surface with chopped parsley.

SERVING SUGGESTION: Plenty of crisp-crusted sourdough bread is a must for this.

WINE: This is one of the few fish dishes that is traditionally served with a light fruity red wine, but I find one of the new varietal rosés, such as a Pinot Noir or Zinfandel rosé, works beautifully.

Baked Petrale with White Wine

CASTAGNOLA'S

Petrale is the finest of the Pacific's flatfish, with the possible exception of halibut. It has more flavor than Rex sole, Dover sole, English sole, or flounder. In the East, where you can't get Petrale, use sea bass or any appropriate flatfish fillet.

- 6 fillets of fresh Petrale sole (or sea bass, lemon sole)
- ½ loaf fresh white bread (sandwich bread)
- 1 teaspoon salt

¼ teaspoon pepper
2 tablespoons finely chopped parsley
¼ cup garlic oil (see note)
⅓ cup dry white wine

Rinse and dry the fish fillets. Set them on a plate or a sheet of wax paper until you are ready to bake them. Heat the oven to 400°F. Trim the crust from the bread. Put the white part of the bread in a blender or food processor. Grind the bread into crumbs. Combine the crumbs with the salt, pepper and parsley in a dish. Dip the fillets in the garlic oil, then the bread crumbs. Arrange the fillets on a greased baking sheet. Bake them for 10 minutes.

When the fillets are done, remove them from the oven. Pour the wine into the pan (but not over the fish). It will sizzle and boil on the hot pan. When the sizzling subsides, use a spatula to transfer the fish fillets to a serving platter. Pour the wine sauce over the fish. Serve with lemon.

Makes 6 servings.

NOTE: To make garlic oil, cut 2 garlic cloves in half lengthwise and gently heat them in the oil for 5 minutes, but do not let them brown. Discard the garlic and use the oil.

WINE: A light Chardonnay or dry Chenin Blanc.

Salmon and Shrimp Newberg

SAM'S GRILL

Leave it to an old-time San Francisco restaurant like Sam's to add the utterly unexpected but totally welcome fillip of flaked salmon to a standard American classic like Shrimp Newberg. Clearly a special-occasion dish.

3 pounds fresh salmon (6 steaks or fillets)
1 lemon, sliced
½ cup (1 stick) butter
½ cup flour
1 quart milk, scalded
1 teaspoon salt
½ cup dry sherry
8 ounces cooked bay shrimp

¾ cup grated Parmesan cheese
Dash of paprika
2 tablespoons melted butter

Put the salmon and the lemon slices in a saucepan. Pour in boiling water to cover the fish and let it simmer for 10 minutes. Drain it well, then bone and flake the salmon.

In a medium-size saucepan, melt the butter and stir in the flour. Cook, stirring with a wire whisk, for 2 to 3 minutes, or until the raw-flour aroma dissipates. Pour the hot milk into the roux, stirring until it becomes smooth. Add the salt and the sherry, bring the sauce to a boil briefly, then remove it from the heat. This can be done well in advance.

Heat the oven to 400°F. Pour enough sauce into an ovenproof baking dish or a serving platter with high sides to coat the bottom. Add the flaked salmon and scatter the shrimp evenly over the top. Cover with the rest of the sauce. Sprinkle the surface with grated Parmesan cheese, paprika, and the melted butter. Bake the dish until the surface is golden brown, 5 to 10 minutes. Serve it with rice.

Makes 6 servings.

WINE: Serve this with a rich Chardonnay or a white Burgundy.

Sole Delmonico

SPENGER'S FISH GROTTO

Thin fillets of sole sandwich a layer of spinach, and instead of a delicate sauce we have a hearty one redolent with smoky bacon and sharp Parmesan cheese. It seems like it shouldn't, but it works.

12 fillets of sole, about 3 ounces each
1½ pounds fresh spinach, finely chopped
French bread crumbs
4 cups Bechamel sauce (see recipe below)
4 tablespoons Parmesan cheese, grated
8 slices bacon, browned and finely chopped
6 ounces bay shrimp

Pat the fish fillets dry and arrange half of them flat in a baking pan. Heat the oven to 425°F.

Cook the spinach in a couple of tablespoons of water for 2 minutes. Add enough bread crumbs to make a fairly heavy mixture, one that holds together when you pick some up with a spoon. Divide the spinach mixture among the 6 fillets, spreading it evenly to cover the surface.

Place a second fillet of sole over each piece of spinach-topped sole to make a sandwich. Brush the surface with melted butter and bake it for 25 minutes.

Make the Bechamel (cream sauce) with ¼ cup butter and ⅓ cup flour to 4 cups of milk. Let it simmer for 5 minutes, then add the cheese, bacon, and shrimp. Remove the fish from the oven, ladle the sauce over it, and serve it.

Makes 6 servings.

SERVING SUGGESTION: Something crisp, like fried potatoes, or glazed carrots, is all the accompaniment it can use.

WINE: Sauvignon Blanc or a white Graves works well with the smoky taste of the bacon.

Sole Soufflé au Champagne

LE RHÔNE

Fresh fish is an absolute must to make the soufflé mixture, or it won't hold together. Keep the fish warm by covering it with foil as you make the sauce. Don't try to keep the fish warm in the oven or it will dry out.

6 whole fish (rock cod, yellowtail), about 1 pound each
2 pounds fillet of sole, must be fresh
2 egg whites
¼ teaspoon white pepper
1 teaspoon salt
1½ cups heavy cream, divided
1 tablespoon chopped truffle (optional)
3 shallots, chopped
2 cups Champagne (can be leftover)

Clean and skin the whole fish and set them aside. In a food processor, purée the fillets, egg whites, white pepper, salt, ½ cup of the heavy cream, and truffle. Make this very smooth, and fill the cavities of the whole fish with it.

Heat the oven to 400°F. Place the fish in a baking pan (or pans) large enough to accommodate them without overlapping them. Sprinkle them with a little salt, the chopped shallots, and the Champagne. Cover the pan and bake them for 15 minutes.

In a wide, flat pan (the wider the better to speed up the reduction process), put 1 cup of the pan juices from the fish and boil it down to about ¼ cup. Add the remaining cup of cream and boil it to reduce it by half. Glaze the fish with sauce and serve any remaining sauce in a sauceboat.

Makes 6 servings.

SERVING SUGGESTION: Chopped spinach or sorrel lightly sautéed in butter with a squirt of lemon makes a perfect accompanying vegetable. Toss it lightly for 1 minute in a second skillet while the cream reduces into the sauce.

WINE: Champagne, of course, or a Pinot Blanc.

Sole Vanessi

SARDINE FACTORY

This is a perfect dish as a fish course in a more complicated meal because so much of it can be done in advance. The fish can be rolled up, the sauce made and poured over the fish, and kept covered at room temperature up to an hour before popping it into the oven to bake.

The Fish:
6 fillets of sole (3 ounces each)
3 slices (4 ounces) Swiss cheese, halved lengthwise
1 package (6 ounces) frozen crab meat, thawed, or 1 cup fresh
½ teaspoon dried basil, crushed
6 small mushroom caps

The Sauce:
2 tablespoons butter
2 tablespoons chopped mushrooms (1 large or 2 medium mushrooms)
½ teaspoon chopped shallots (½ small shallot)
1½ teaspoons lemon juice

3 tablespoons dry white wine
2 tablespoons clarified butter (or melted butter)
3 tablespoons flour
1 cup fish broth (or clam juice)
⅓ cup half-and-half

Place the fish on a work surface skin side up. On each fillet place a half slice of Swiss cheese, an ounce of crab meat, a pinch of basil, and a mushroom cap. Roll them up and place them in a casserole or glass baking dish, seam side down. Heat the oven to 400°F.

In a saucepan, heat the butter and cook the mushrooms, shallots, 1 teaspoon of the lemon juice, and the wine until the wine has evaporated. Add the butter and the flour. Mix it well, then add the fish broth. Cook and stir the sauce until it is thickened and bubbling. Add the cream, the remaining ½ teaspoon of lemon juice, and salt to taste. Pour the sauce over the fish rolls. Bake them for 16 to 20 minutes, covered, until the fish is opaque when tested with a fork.

Makes 6 servings.

SERVING SUGGESTION: As a fish course in the context of a larger meal, garnish it with cut lemon. As a light luncheon dish, it goes nicely with lightly sautéed zucchini and carrots.

WINE: Chenin Blanc or a light Chardonnay.

Sole Chambertin

LA BOURGOGNE

Fish in red wine is not such a strange idea; it's been done for centuries, which ought to put the lie to some snobbish ideas about fish and white wine. The addition of brown sauce, while unusual in this day, is actually classic in French cuisine.

6 fillets of sole (about 1 pound)
1 cup red wine
2 medium shallots, chopped
½ cup demi-glace (or brown gravy)
½ cup butter

Distribute the sole fillets in a large nonaluminum skillet. (Aluminum reacts with wine to add a metallic flavor.) Pour in the red wine and shallots, cover the pan and bring it to a boil. Immediately lower the heat to let it simmer until the fish is done, 5 minutes or less for the average fillet, more for thicker onces, less for thinner ones. Drain the fish and arrange it on a serving platter.

Turn up the heat under the wine and reduce it by half. Add the demi-glace or brown gravy, bring it to a boil, and immediately remove it from the heat. Swirl in the butter and strain the sauce over the fish.

Makes 6 servings as the fish course in a multi-course meal; 3 servings otherwise.

SERVING SUGGESTION: Crisp fried potatoes, preceded or followed by a green salad.

WINE: A dry varietal rosé or a Pinot Noir Blanc.

Coulibiac in Brioche

CALIFORNIA CULINARY ACADEMY

When you cut into this and expose the filling with its pink salmon, white rice, yellow eggs, and brown mushrooms wrapped in a golden brioche dough, the oohs and aahs from assembled guests will be exceeded only by the exclamations upon taking the first bite. The combination is a classic.

The Salmon:
2½ pounds salmon fillet
Juice of 2 lemons
2 tablespoons dry dill weed

The Dough:
1 package active dry yeast
¼ cup lukewarm water (110°F)
½ cup butter
1 tablespoon sugar
1 teaspoon salt
3 eggs

½ cup lukewarm milk
3 to 4 cups flour

The Filling:
3 egg yolks
Salt, white pepper
Dry dill weed
1 cup sour cream
1½ cups cooked rice
3 hard-cooked eggs
1 pound mushrooms, sliced
3 to 4 tablespoons butter

Put the salmon in a glass or ceramic pan. Add the lemon juice and the dill weed. Marinate the salmon, refrigerated, for 24 hours, turning it occasionally.

Make the dough next. Dissolve the yeast in the warm water in a small bowl. In a large bowl, beat the butter with the sugar and salt until it is smooth. Beat in the eggs and the milk. When it is quite smooth, stir in the yeast mixture. Work in enough flour to make a soft dough. Turn it out onto a floured board and knead it until it is smooth. Let it rise until it doubles in bulk, punch it down, wrap it tightly in plastic or a moist cloth, and keep it refrigerated.

Prepare the filling ingredients. Beat the yolks with 1 teaspoon of salt, a pinch of white pepper, a bit of dill, and the sour cream. Mix in the rice. Set it aside. Shell and quarter the eggs. Set them aside. Sauté the mushrooms in the butter just long enough to brown them lightly. Set them aside.

To assemble the Coulibiac, roll out half the brioche dough into a long rectangle. It is traditional to trim this into the shape of a fish, but it is not necessary. Drain the salmon and pat it dry. Spoon half the rice mixture on the dough, leaving a margin of 1 inch all the way around. Lay the salmon fillets on the rice. Arrange the hard-cooked egg quarters around the salmon. Make a wide row of mushrooms on top of the salmon. Spoon the remaining rice mixture between the eggs and around the mushrooms. Roll out the remaining dough the same size and shape as the bottom. Put it on top of the fish, crimp the top and bottom edges, and seal it with egg wash (1 egg beaten with 1 tablespoon milk).

Make a 1-inch hole as a vent (if the dough is cut in the shape of fish, make it the eye). You may also decorate the package with bits of the brioche dough—for a fish-shaped package, cut small pieces to look like fins, and score the "body" to resemble scales. Chill the package at least 10 minutes to firm the dough.

Heat the oven to 325°F. Brush the surface of the package with the remaining egg wash. Bake it for 1 hour, 15 minutes, or until it is golden brown. To serve it, slice it crosswise.

Makes 6 servings.

SERVING SUGGESTION: A sauce velouté based on a fumet (fishstock) made from the salmon bones is magnificent draped over each serving. Follow it with a vegetable salad or precede it with a vegetable soup, because a vegetable served with it tends to detract from its glory.

WINE: A great Sauvignon Blanc or Pouilly-Fumé.

Trout à l'Orange

CAFÉ MOZART

A variation of the "en papillote" theme, this is an easy way to deal with trout. The packages can be made up hours in advance and just popped under the broiler at the last minute.

For Each Serving:

1 trout, 10 to 12 ounces
1 teaspoon butter
1 square sheet aluminum foil
Salt, pepper
Juice of ¼ lemon
Juice of ¼ orange
1 jumbo prawn (shrimp), shelled, or a baby
    lobster tail
1 thin slice lemon
2 thin slices orange
1 sprig parsley
½ teaspoon butter

Pat the trout dry with a paper towel. Butter the sheet of aluminum foil and place the trout near the center of the foil, but slightly off center. Sprinkle the fish, including the cavity, with salt and pepper and citrus juices. Lay a prawn on top of the fish and surround it with the remaining ingredients. Close up the package by folding the foil in half and sealing the edges by crimping them back on themselves.

Heat the broiler. Put the package(s) of trout on a baking sheet and set them under the broiler flame on the lowest position (farthest from the flame). Cook for

10 minutes. The foil packages will puff up like a balloon. Carefully open the packages and serve the trout with the accumulated juices. (If you want to be fancy, you can bone the trout at the table like a maitre d'—just pull out the backbone and the smaller bones come out with it. It's easy to do; each person can bone his own).

SERVING SUGGESTION: As a fish course in a larger meal, slices of orange and lemon are sufficient. As a light luncheon or supper, complement it with crisp fried potatoes and a salad.

WINE: A dry or slightly off-dry White Riesling picks up the citrus flavors appealingly.

Trout Maison

ROBERT

If you don't start the sauce before you bake the fish, you will have to be content to let the fish cool practically to room temperature while you patiently reduce the sauce. It can take up to 30 minutes. Use the widest pan you have to speed up the process. The more surface you expose to the heat, the faster the sauce will form.

The Poaching Liquid:
1 tablespoon butter
4 shallots, finely chopped
2 bay leaves
6 sprigs parsley
4 cups dry white wine (or 1 bottle, 750 ml.)
3 cups water
Juice of 1 lemon
2 teaspoons salt
½ teaspoon pepper

The Sauce:
2 cups strained poaching liquid
2 more shallots, finely chopped
1 cup heavy cream
½ cup unsalted butter
Juice of ½ lemon
Salt, white pepper

The Fish:
6 trout, cleaned but left whole (about 10 to 12 ounces each)

Combine the ingredients for the poaching liquid in a saucepan and bring them to a boil. Let them simmer 10 minutes, covered. Meanwhile, heat the oven to 400°F. Arrange the trout in the bottom of a casserole or baking dish.

Strain 2 cups of the poaching liquid into another saucepan. Combine the strained liquid with the shallots for the sauce, bring them to a boil and continue boiling until the liquid reduces to ⅔ cup. Set it aside.

Pour the hot poaching liquid (from the original pan) over the trout, cover the pan and bake the fish for 10 minutes. Check the fish to see if they are cooked; they may need a few more minutes if the trout are large. When they are done, skin them and place them on a serving platter or individual plates. Keep the rest warm as you work on each one.

Meanwhile, return the pan with the reduced poaching liquid and shallots to a high flame, add the cream and reduce it again to ¾ cup. It will form into a very light sauce, just thick enough to coat the spoon. Off the heat, stir in the butter and lemon juice, stirring continuously to keep it smooth. Add salt and pepper to taste and strain the sauce over the fish.

Makes 6 servings.

SERVING SUGGESTION: A prime requisite is crusty French bread to sop up the sauce. With a crisp salad, this makes a lovely lunch or late supper.

WINE: A light Pouilly-Fumé or Sauvignon Blanc.

NOTE: It helps the texture of the sauce if you select a white wine of considerable acidity, such as a Chablis (French), Muscadet, or Champagne (sparkling or still wine). The more the wine makes your mouth pucker, the better it is for this dish.

Trout C.C.A.

CALIFORNIA CULINARY ACADEMY

The chefs and students at this new chef's school in San Francisco came up with this nouvelle cuisine dish for one of their daily dinner menus. Needless to say, it was a hit. Like most nouvelle cuisine dishes, it involves quite a bit of last-minute preparation. It is an ideal dish for two people to work on together—one to deal with the fish, the other to perfect the sauce, a delicate rascal that demands patience and attention.

The Poaching Liquid:
3 cups dry white wine
3 cups water
1 onion, quartered
2 or 3 cloves
1 bay leaf
Pinch of thyme
5 or 6 peppercorns

The Vin Blanc Sauce:
¼ cup finely chopped shallots
1 cup dry white wine
2 cups heavy cream
4 tablespoons softened butter
Salt, white pepper

The Garnish:
2 cups julienne-cut leeks
2 cups julienne-cut celery
2 cups julienne-cut carrot
1 quart water
1 tablespoon salt

The Fish:
6 whole dressed trout, 10 to 12 ounces each

Combine the ingredients for the poaching liquid in a saucepan. Cover it and let it boil for 30 minutes.

Meanwhile, in another pan, prepare the base of the vin blanc sauce. Cook the shallots in the white wine until the wine reduces by half. Add the cream and let it boil until it reduces by half again. Keep the sauce warm until it is ready to serve.

Blanch the leeks, celery, and carrot in salted water. (Cut the vegetables into thin "matchsticks" about 2 inches long. Bring the water to a boil with the salt. Drop the vegetables into the water for 60 to 90 seconds.) When they begin to wilt, but before they lose their bright colors, drain them.

All of the above steps can be done up to 2 hours in advance.

Place the trout in a large frying pan, belly down. Strain the hot poaching liquid over the trout, bring it to a simmer, cover the pan, and let it simmer gently for 7 minutes, or until the fish is cooked. (Test by checking the flesh at the tail of one of the fish; it should be opaque all the way through.) As the trout finishes cooking, reheat the sauce, swirl in the butter and season it to taste with salt and pepper.

Drain the trout well when it is finished cooking, and place it in the middle of a dinner plate, belly down. Ladle some of the sauce all around the trout in a thin ribbon on the plate. Drape the garnish over the trout's back.

Makes 6 servings.

SERVING SUGGESTION: Boiled potatoes and a fresh green vegetable.

WINE: A light Chardonnay.

Braised Fish Hunan Style

TAI CHI

Unless you have an oversized restaurant wok big enough to hold a whole fish comfortably, this alternative and decidedly non-Chinese method for cooking the fish is much easier to handle and produces a finished dish just as delicious as the "right" way. The Chinese method is to cook the fish in oil in the wok until it is done, then drain the oil and add the remaining ingredients to make a sauce. With this alternative method, which I have adapted from Tai Chi's recipe, the fish is baked in the oven, topped by the same delicious sauce.

1 rockfish or grouper, 3 to 4 pounds, head and tail intact
2 to 3 tablespoons vegetable oil
1 clove garlic, finely chopped
1 thin slice fresh ginger root, finely chopped
¼ cup each:
  shredded carrot
  shredded black mushrooms (soaked and drained)
  shredded water chestnuts
  shredded bamboo shoots
  shredded Szechwan pickled vegetable
2 tablespoons soy sauce
1 teaspoon crushed red pepper
⅓ cup chicken broth
1 tablespoon sesame oil

Heat the oven to 425°F. Coat the fish with vegetable oil and place it in a baking pan large enough to hold it flat. Bake the fish 15 minutes, or until it is done. (A fish 1½ inches thick at its thickest point will take 15 minutes; figure 10 minutes per inch of thickness.)

While the fish cooks, heat 1 tablespoon oil in a wok. Stir-fry the ginger and garlic for a few seconds, then add the shredded vegetables. Stir-fry them for 1 minute, then add the soy sauce, red pepper, and chicken broth. Boil for 1 minute.

When the fish is done, place it on a serving platter. Add the sesame oil to the sauce and spoon it over the fish.

Makes 6 servings.

Poultry

Chicken in Mustard

CAFÉ MOZART

The first time I tasted this dish, the restaurant served the boneless chicken cut into bite-size chunks, prepared with the same sauce and served over vol-au-vents (puff pastry rings). Like most sautéed dishes, this really works best when prepared for 1 or 2 servings.

For Each Serving:
1 tablespoon butter
1 shallot, finely chopped
Salt, pepper
1 boneless breast of chicken
1 tablespoon Calvados or applejack
¼ cup heavy cream
1 tablespoon stoneground mustard
1 egg yolk, beaten

Melt the butter in a sauté pan with the shallot. Lightly salt and pepper the chicken breast. Sauté it 3 minutes on each side over moderate heat, turning once only. Remove the chicken and keep it warm while you make the sauce. Add the Calvados to the pan and scrape up any bits of chicken to dissolve them. Add the cream and the mustard, let the sauce simmer for a few seconds, then quickly stir in the yolk to thicken it. Immediately, pour the sauce over the chicken.

SERVING SUGGESTION: Boiled rice to soak up the lovely sauce, zucchini cut in thin slices sautéed in butter for 2 minutes then finished with a sprinkle of salt and a squirt of fresh lemon juice to taste.

WINE: Alsatian Riesling or a California Chenin Blanc.

Chicken Jerusalem

JACK'S

Chicken with artichoke hearts and mushrooms is a San Francisco classic, but it shows up in all kinds of variations. The original, according to historians, is Jack's Chicken Jerusalem. Purportedly, this was made with sliced Jerusalem artichokes, a crisp, starchy vegetable that is not even related to the more familiar globe artichoke. Jack's makes its Chicken Jerusalem today with globe artichoke hearts, although I have tried the recipe with Jerusalem artichokes and it has a totally different and special character. The variations are distinct—among them, Poulet Mascotte bases its sauce on (red) Zinfandel wine, and Chicken Elizabeth does it with brown sauce, while Jack's original is based on cream. The differences are fascinating, and I have included all three for comparison.

For Each Serving:

2 tablespoons butter
1 large chicken breast, boned and halved
6 medium mushrooms
4 medium artichoke hearts
2 tablespoons dry sherry
¾ cup half-and-half
2 egg yolks
1½ teaspoons lemon juice
¼ teaspoon salt
Pinch of freshly ground black pepper
½ teaspoon chopped chives for garnish

Melt the butter in a skillet large enough to hold the chicken breasts in one layer, and which also has a cover. Over moderate heat, brown the chicken evenly on both sides. Cover the pan, reduce the heat and cook the chicken slowly for 15 minutes, or until it is just barely cooked through. Remove the chicken from the pan.

Raise the heat under the pan. Brown the mushrooms and artichokes hearts in the remaining fat. Add the sherry and let it simmer until the wine has just about evaporated. Keep scraping the bottom of the pan to dissolve any browned bits. Add the half-and-half. When it comes to a boil, remove it from the heat.

In a small bowl, beat the yolks and lemon juice. Slowly stir some of the hot sauce from the pan into the egg yolks, stirring constantly until it is smooth. Return the mixture to the pan, stirring constantly. Add the salt and pepper and return the pan to the heat. Lower the flame and let it cook until the sauce is hot. Do not let it boil. Return the chicken to the pan to heat through. Serve the chicken with chives sprinkled over the top.

SERVING SUGGESTION: White rice to catch the sauce is all this needs. The same is true of the succeeding versions.

WINE: A fruity white wine, such as Chenin Blanc or White Riesling.

Poulet Mascotte

CARNELIAN ROOM

2 whole chickens, disjointed
Salt, pepper
Flour
4 tablespoons butter, melted
½ shallot, finely chopped
1 cup Zinfandel wine
2 cups chicken broth
3 tablespoons tomato paste
Pinch of thyme
4 medium artichoke bottoms, quartered
1 pound mushrooms, cut in half
1 pound potatoes, peeled and trimmed into olive shapes
2 tablespoons butter
2 tablespoons flour

Season the chicken lightly with salt and pepper. Dredge the pieces in flour, shaking off the excess. Brown the chicken in the melted butter. Do not crowd the pan; do the chicken in shifts if necessary. When the chicken is brown, put it in a large casserole. Meanwhile, heat the oven to 375°F.

Add the shallot and wine to the pan. Let it boil, scraping up the browned bits left in the pan to dissolve them. Stir in the tomato paste. Pour the wine and the chicken broth over the chicken in the casserole. Add the tomato paste, thyme, artichoke bottoms, mushrooms, and potatoes to the casserole. Bake it for 1 hour.

Arrange the chicken on a serving platter. Thicken the sauce in the casserole with a roux made by mashing together the 2 tablespoons of butter and flour. Bring it to a boil and pour it over the chicken.

Makes 6 servings.

Chicken Elizabeth

SAM'S GRILL

For 2 Servings:
1 frying chicken, disjointed

2 tablespoons butter
2 tablespoons oil
3 scallions, finely chopped
½ green pepper, seeded and finely chopped
¼ pound mushrooms, sliced
¼ cup dry white wine
½ cup brown gravy (or demi-glace sauce if you
    have it)
4 artichoke hearts, cooked and cut in half

In a heavy skillet, over fairly high heat, brown the chicken in the butter and oil, turning it to brown it on all sides. When it is golden brown, add the scallions, green pepper, and mushrooms, shaking the pan and turning the chicken to keep it from sticking. Add the wine and let it boil for 2 minutes. Add the gravy and cover the pan. Turn down the heat and let it simmer until the chicken is done, about 20 to 30 minutes, depending on the size of the chicken.

When the chicken is almost done, add the artichoke hearts to heat through.

Makes 6 servings.

Chicken à la Ritz

RITZ OLD POODLE DOG

The cream curdles as the chicken simmers, but don't worry. The addition of egg yolks at the end smooths out the sauce of the Poodle Dog's signature dish.

2 frying chickens, about 2½ pounds each,
    disjointed
6 tablespoons butter
½ pound mushrooms, sliced
3 scallions, finely chopped
1 cup dry white wine
2 cups half-and-half
4 egg yolks
Salt, pepper

Brown the chicken in the butter in two skillets until it turns a golden yellow. Keep turning the chicken to brown it evenly. Add the mushrooms, scallions, wine, and half-and-half, dividing it between the pans. Bring it to a boil, reduce the heat and let it simmer until the chicken is cooked, 15 to 20 minutes.

Beat the yolks in a large mixing bowl. Drain the cooking juices into the yolks and beat the mixture with a wire whisk until it is smooth. Divide the mixture between the two pans and heat the sauce gently, stirring it until it thickens lightly. Do not let it boil.

Makes 6 servings.

SERVING SUGGESTION: Serve the chicken with wild rice. This needs a simply prepared green vegetable, such as boiled asparagus, broccoli, snow peas or spinach. A spinach salad following it makes a lovely contrast.

WINE: Sauvignon Blanc or Pouilly-Fumé.

Chicken San Joaquin

GOLDEN EAGLE

The pure flavors of tomato, olive, mushrooms, and shallots hark to the Mediterranean (Italian, Spanish) heritage of California's great Central Valley. It translates to a simple, easy to prepare casserole.

6 half chicken breasts
6 chicken legs
6 chicken thighs
Salt, pepper
⅔ cup olive oil
1½ cups dry white wine
¾ pound mushrooms, sliced
⅓ cup finely chopped shallots
1½ cups pitted ripe olives
3 cups chopped fresh or canned tomatoes

Heat the oven to 375°F. Have ready a casserole large enough to hold the chicken and the vegetables. Lightly salt and pepper the chicken.

In a large skillet, heat the olive oil and brown the chicken in it. Do not crowd the pan. Do the chicken in shifts if necessary. When it has browned, put it in the casserole. Pour off the oil and reserve it. Deglaze the pan with the white wine (bring it to a boil and scrape up any browned bits that adhere to the bottom of the pan to dissolve them). Pour the wine into the casserole.

Return the reserved oil to the skillet along with the mushrooms and shallots. Sauté them until the mushrooms have browned. Drain the fat and add the mushrooms and shallots to the casserole along with the olives and tomatoes. Cover the casserole and bake it for 45 minutes.

Makes 6 servings.

SERVING SUGGESTION: Baked or fried potatoes, or rice, and a fresh green vegetable.

WINE: A light red, such as a light Zinfandel, Gamay, or Bardolino.

Poularde au Champagne

DOMAINE CHANDON

The secret to flour-less nouvelle cuisine sauces is patience. It takes longer than you might think to reduce the liquid, then the cream, to the proper consistency, but patience is crucial to the success of this dish. Keep the chicken loosely covered with foil next to the stove while you reduce the wine first, then the cream. What happens, in technical terms, is that the acidity of the wine increases as it evaporates; this acid combines with the butterfat in the cream, the moisture from which evaporates to concentrate the butterfat. The sauce actually emulsifies, the same basic principle as mayonnaise or hollandaise, except that this one must boil to form the emulsion. The texture of the sauce is noticeably lighter and more velvety than those thickened with starch.

    2 frying chickens, 2½ to 3 pounds each
    2 tablespoons butter
    2 tablespoons oil
    6 shallots, finely chopped
    2 cups dry (brut) champagne
    2 cups heavy cream

Clean the chickens and cut them into serving pieces. Pat them dry with a towel. Sauté the chicken pieces in the butter and oil in a heavy skillet over moderate heat. Do not crowd the pan; do the chickens in two pans if necessary, or in two shifts. Cook the chicken until it is nicely browned and cooked through, about 25 minutes in all. Remove the chicken from the pan and set it aside. Do not put it in the oven to keep warm, as this will dry it out.

Pour the grease from the pan. Add the shallots and the wine. Turn up the heat and scrape up any browned bits that may adhere to the bottom of the pan to dissolve them. Boil the wine until it is reduced to about ⅓ cup. It should have the consistency of a light syrup. Add the cream and let it boil until it reduces by half and thickens into a light sauce. Add the chicken during the final stages of this reduction to reheat it, about 3 to 5 minutes. Taste the sauce for salt and pepper. Serve the chicken napped with the sauce.

Makes 6 servings.

SERVING SUGGESTION: Lightly sautéed 2-inch strips of zucchini or summer squash, green beans or Brussels sprouts.

WINE: A dry Champagne or California sparkling wine, of course.

NOTE: Canned morel mushrooms may be added to the sauce when you add the chicken for an elegant additional touch.

Chicken with Pears and Endives

ERNIE'S

Straight out of nouvelle cuisine, Chef Jacky Robert's creation blends the sweetness of ripe pears with the pleasant bitterness of Belgian endive in a lovely sauce. The pear purée gives the sauce its body; no flour or other thickener is necessary.

For 2 Servings:
    1 chicken, 3 to 3½ pounds
    2 pears
    2 cups chicken broth
    Salt, pepper
    1 cup heavy cream
    2 heads Belgian endive

Skin and disjoint the chicken. Peel the pears, reserving the peel. Core the pears, cut them in chunks, and poach the pears in the chicken broth, uncovered, until they are tender. Drain the pears, reserving the broth.

Purée the pears in a food processor or a blender and set them aside.

In a vegetable steamer, combine the pear-flavored broth and the pear peelings. Bring them to a simmer. Sprinkle the chicken with salt and pepper, put it in the top of the steamer, cover it and let it steam for 15 to 20 minutes, or just until it is done.

Meanwhile, put the cream in a saucepan and turn the heat on under it. Reserve six endive leaves and finely chop the rest. Add the chopped endive to the cream and let it boil until the liquid reduces to ½ cup. Add the pear purée, heat it through and strain the sauce if you want it to be smooth. (If you like the chunks of endive in it, don't strain it.) If the sauce seems too thick, add a little of the steaming liquid. When the chicken is done, serve it with the sauce and garnished with the reserved endive leaves.

Makes 2 servings.

SERVING SUGGESTION: A little cherry tomato or carrot for color contrast, and crusty French bread to soak up every last drop of the wonderful sauce.

WINE: A rich Chardonnay, Sauvignon Blanc, or White Burgundy.

Chicken Gloria

AU RELAIS

Sonoma County, north of San Francisco, is covered with fruit and nut trees, wherever there are no grapevines. Walnuts and apricots dominate. Nearby Petaluma raises the best chickens in the state, which makes a dish combining the three inevitable. It is frankly sweet due to the apricot syrup, which is necessary to give the sauce body.

6 chicken drumsticks
6 supremes (half of a boned breast of chicken)
Salt, pepper
Flour
6 tablespoons butter
1½ cups medium dry sherry
1½ cups crushed walnuts

1½ cups heavy cream
3 dozen apricot halves (canned in heavy syrup)

Season the chicken pieces with salt and pepper. Dredge them in flour. Heat the oven to 400°F. Melt the butter in a large frying pan. Brown the chicken in the butter, in two shifts to keep from crowding the pan. Arrange the chicken pieces in a baking pan, skin side down. Bake the chicken 10 minutes, turn the pieces over and bake another 5 minutes.

Pour off the fat. Add the sherry to the pan, then walnuts, the cream, and the apricots and their syrup. Bake 5 minutes longer, basting the chicken once or twice with the sauce. Serve it immediately with a green vegetable.

Makes 6 servings.

WINE: An off-dry Chenin Blanc, Johannesberg Riesling or Rheingau.

NOTE: This is an ideal dish to make 1 or 2 servings. For each serving allow a leg and a supreme, 1 tablespoon of butter for browning, ¼ cup each crushed walnuts, sherry, and cream. Use 6 apricot halves per serving.

Sesame Chicken

YAMATO

The combination of a ginger-spiked marinade and a crisp coating with the flavor of sesame seeds gives this Japanese chicken dish its special character. For the full recipe (6 servings) it's much easier to use a deep-fryer, otherwise haul out the biggest frying pan you have.

½ cup soy sauce
2 tablespoons sugar
2 tablespoons sake or dry sherry
½ teaspoon grated ginger root
2 chickens, about 2½ to 3 pounds each, hacked into 1½-inch pieces
½ cup cornstarch
2 tablespoons toasted sesame seeds
2 cups oil

Blend the soy sauce, sugar, sake, and ginger root. Toss the chicken pieces in this marinade and let it sit for 30 to 40 minutes. Combine the cornstarch and sesame seeds in a bowl or a large plate. Dredge the chicken pieces in the mixture. (Or use a paper bag; put the cornstarch and sesame in the bag; toss the chicken pieces in the bag). Let the pieces sit for 10 minutes.

In a frying pan or deep-fryer heat the oil to 360 to 370°F. Fry the chicken until it is golden brown, about 5 minutes for boneless chicken, 8 to 10 minutes for chicken with bone. Do not overfill the pan. Do the chicken in shifts. Serve the chicken with little bowls of soy sauce and hot mustard for dipping.

Makes 6 servings.

WINE: Sake or beer is better, although a light Sauvignon Blanc works nicely.

NOTE: For 2 servings, use 1 whole chicken breast, hacked into 1½-inch pieces, the full amount of marinade, but half the quantities of cornstarch and sesame seeds.

Almond Chicken

KAN'S

If the current swing toward Mandarin dishes and away from Cantonese cuisine has captured you, consider the delicate majesty of this simple dish. Because there are no strong flavors to cover up any flaws, use only the best ingredients. Fry the almonds first, then use some of the drained oil to sauté the chicken.

3 tablespoons oil
½ teaspoon salt
1 whole boneless breast from a 3-pound chicken, cut into 1-inch cubes
½ cup each:
    diced water chestnuts
    diced bamboo shoots
    diced celery
    diced mushrooms
½ cup chicken broth
1 teaspoon soy sauce
2 tablespoons cornstarch
2 tablespoons water

½ cup whole shelled almonds, browned in oil and drained

Heat the wok over a high flame for 30 seconds. Add the oil and salt, bring it to a sizzle, then add the chicken. Stir-fry it over high heat until the chicken is almost done, about 3 minutes. Reduce the heat and add the water chestnuts, bamboo shoots, celery, and mushrooms. Stir-fry the vegetables and chicken to mix them evenly; add the chicken broth and soy sauce. Cover the pan and let it cook for 1 minute.

Mix the cornstarch and water to make a thin paste. Uncover the wok and stir this paste into the sauce. Cook, stirring, until the sauce thickens. Turn the mixture out in a mound on a serving plate. Garnish it with the fried almonds.

Makes 2 servings as a main dish by itself, 6 servings in the context of a Chinese meal of several courses.

WINE: French Colombard or Chenin Blanc.

Lemon Chicken

MARRAKECH

As with other Moroccan dishes, this is designed to be eaten with the fingers (of the right hand only). Therefore, the chicken must be cooked to the point where it can be easily pulled from the bone. To give the sauce a bit more zip, some Moroccan cooks like to add the lemons to the liquid as it reduces to flavor the sauce with them.

¼ cup oil
½ cup (1 stick) butter
1 medium onion, coarsely chopped
½ teaspoon saffron
½ teaspoon ground ginger
½ teaspoon salt
2 teaspoons pepper
1 frying chicken, about 3 pounds, split lengthwise
1 lemon
½ teaspoon salt
½ cup white wine vinegar (or more)

Use a sauté pan or a wide saucepan with a cover large enough to accommodate the chicken halves. Heat the oil and the butter in the pan over moderate heat. Add the onion, saffron, ginger, salt, and pepper. Cook it until the onion softens, then put the chicken in skin-side down to brown it lightly. Turn the chicken skin-side up, add 2 cups water, and cover the pan. Let the chicken simmer for 1½ hours.

Meanwhile, cut the lemon in half and squeeze the juice into a stainless steel or ceramic saucepan. (Do not use aluminum, which will discolor the lemon.) Cut the rind into eighths. Put the lemon rind, salt, and enough vinegar to cover the rind in the saucepan. Boil the mixture for 20 minutes. Drain it.

When the chicken is done, remove it from the pan and place it on a serving platter. Turn the heat up under the remaining juices and reduce them to 1 cup. Strain the sauce over the chicken and garnish it with the pickled lemon rind.

Makes 2 large or 4 small servings.

WINE: The lemon competes with any subtleties in wine. A jug white would be all right, beer better.

Tung-An Chicken

TAI CHI

Hot and sour are the dominant flavors of this Hunanese dish. Adjust the red pepper to your taste, but I advise beginning with the lower amount. You don't want to burn your guests' lips.

1 whole chicken breast
⅓ cup tree ears (wood ear)
⅓ cup zucchini
⅓ cup bamboo shoots
⅓ cup chicken broth
1 tablespoon Hsao Hsing wine or dry sherry
1 tablespoon cider vinegar
1 teaspoon salt
1 teaspoon sugar
1½ tablespoons soy sauce
1½ teaspoons cornstarch dissolved in a small
    amount of cold water
2 tablespoons oil
1 clove garlic, finely chopped
1 thin slice fresh ginger root, finely chopped

1 teaspoon to 1 tablespoon crushed red pepper
1 teaspoon sesame oil

Slice the chicken breast thinly into pieces 1 inch by 2 inches. Soak the wood ear in hot water for 15 minutes, then drain it. Cut the zucchini and bamboo shoots into thin slices. In a small bowl, combine the broth, wine, vinegar, salt, sugar, and soy sauce. Prepare the cornstarch-water paste and set it aside.

In a wok or a large skillet, heat the oil. Fry the garlic and ginger in it for a few seconds until it begins to turn brown, then add the chicken. Stir-fry it for a few seconds until its entire surface has turned white, then add the wood ear, zucchini, and bamboo shoots. Add the red pepper (use the smaller amount the first time to determine whether you really want it any hotter), and stir-fry the chicken with the vegetables for 10 seconds. Add the liquid mixture, cover the wok, and let the mixture stew for 2 minutes.

When the vegetables are done, stir in the cornstarch paste to thicken the sauce. Just before serving, sprinkle the sesame oil over the surface.

Makes 2 servings as a main dish by itself, 6 servings in the context of a Chinese meal of several courses.

SERVING SUGGESTION: Steamed rice, of course. In a Chinese meal of several courses, this is served near the end, just before the fish.

WINE: Since this is a hot and sour dish, beer is a better choice than wine.

Chicken Tabaka

CARAVANSARY

Until I encountered it at this Middle Eastern restaurant, I had never tasted chicken prepared this way. The flavors are bright and savory, and the chicken takes on the most beautiful purple color from the marinade-cooking liquid. It's even good cold the next day, especially sandwiched in the pocket of a pita bread.

6 boned whole breasts of chicken, with the
    wishbone in
½ cup chopped parsley
½ cup chopped coriander (cilantro)
½ cup butter, melted
½ tablespoon oregano leaves

6 to 8 cloves garlic, chopped
1½ teaspoons salt
1½ teaspoons pepper
1 tablespoon flour
½ cup lemon juice
1½ to 2 cups chicken broth
½ cup catsup
½ cup pomegranate juice (see note)

Flatten the chicken breasts slightly so they are of uniform thickness. In a large bowl, combine all the remaining ingredients to make a sauce. Pour half the sauce into a roasting pan just large enough to hold all the chicken breasts without overlapping them. Place the chicken breasts over the sauce and pour the remaining sauce over them. Marinate them overnight, or, better, at least 24 hours, refrigerated.

Weight down the chicken with 3 or 4 heavy plates or a slighty smaller pan weighted down with some full cans of food. Set the pan of chicken over low heat until the sauce comes to a boil. Lower the heat to a simmer and let it cook for 15 minutes. Heat the oven to 350°F. Remove the plates and set the chicken, uncovered, in the oven for 15 minutes longer, basting it occasionally.

Makes 6 servings.

SERVING SUGGESTION: Rice pilaf to catch the marinade-sauce. Fried eggplant slices or sticks make a pleasant contrast.

WINE: A simple red wine, such as Beaujolais, Bardolino, a young Zinfandel, or Gamay.

NOTE: Unsweetened pomegranate juice is available in some health food stores. If it is unavailable, substitute ½ cup dry red wine. Do not use grenadine, as it is sweetened.

Chicken Shahjahani

THE TANDOORI

Indian cuisine offers a riot of flavors and aromas in a single dish, such as this one. The idea of simmering the chicken in a lively sauce based on a purée of onion, ginger root, and tomato sparked with spices such as cinnamon, cardamom, cloves, and cumin is enough to get any lover of spicy food salivating.

1 frying chicken, about 3 pounds
1 cup chopped onions
¾-inch piece fresh ginger root, peeled and
   chopped
2 cloves garlic, chopped
4 medium tomatoes
2 tablespoons oil
1 stick cinnamon, crushed roughly
5 whole cardamom pods
6 whole cloves
2 bay leaves
¼ teaspoon peppercorns
1 teaspoon turmeric
1 teaspoon ground cumin
1½ teaspoons ground coriander seed
1 teaspoon paprika
1 hot green pepper, sliced (optional)
1 pound mushrooms, cleaned and sliced
1 cup water
Pinch of saffron
⅓ cup roasted cashews
⅓ cup slivered almonds
⅓ cup seedless raisins
2 tablespoons chopped coriander leaves (cilantro)

Pull the skin off the chicken. Cut and pull the meat from the bone, cutting it into 1-inch pieces. Dry the meat on towels.

Combine the onions, ginger root, garlic, and tomatoes in a blender. Process them to a purée.

Heat the oil over a fairly high flame in a 4- or 5-quart heavy saucepan until it begins to smoke. Add the cinnamon, cardamom, cloves, bay leaves, and peppercorns and cook for 1 minute. Add the puréed vegetables and boil the mixture for 5 minutes. It should turn slightly brown. Add the turmeric, cumin, coriander seed, paprika, and hot pepper. Cook them for a minute, then add the chicken. Cook, stirring, until the chicken has turned white all over. Add the mushrooms and cook for 3 minutes over reduced heat. Finally, add the remaining ingredients except the chopped coriander and simmer for 10 to 15 minutes, or until the chicken is cooked. Serve the dish sprinkled with chopped coriander.

Makes 6 servings.

SERVING SUGGESTION: Rice, to catch the sauce, is mandatory, of course. Any vegetable dish to serve with this would have to be spicy enough to compete.

WINE: Too spicy for most wines, although a fairly neutral jug white seems to work, as well as beer.

Murghi Masala

INDIA HOUSE

Not as spicy as you might expect, this actually comes off as delicate next to some other Indian dishes. The yogurt acts as a modifying influence.

1 frying chicken, about 3 pounds, disjointed
¼ cup oil
1 large onion, finely chopped
1 stick cinnamon
2 whole cardamom pods (or ½ teaspoon ground cardamom)
2 cloves garlic, finely chopped
Water
1 cup plain yogurt
3 slices (¼ inch each) fresh ginger, peeled and grated
1 teaspoon turmeric
2 teaspoons sweet paprika
1 teaspoon powdered ginger
½ teaspoon cumin powder
1 teaspoon ground coriander seed
Salt
½ cup heavy cream

Pull the skin off the chicken and set it aside.

In a large pot, heat the oil and cook the onion in it until it softens. Add the cinnamon, cardamom, and garlic. Continue cooking until the onion turns golden brown. Add ¼ cup water and the yogurt. Continue cooking, stirring briskly, 5 minutes, then add the fresh ginger, turmeric, paprika, powdered ginger, cumin, and coriander. Stir in 1 cup of water and bring it to a boil.

Add the chicken pieces, reduce the heat and let it simmer for 30 minutes, stirring frequently. Add more water if the liquid boils away. Add salt to taste. Finally add the cream, let it heat through but do not let it boil, and serve the chicken with the coarse sauce.

Makes 6 servings.

SERVING SUGGESTION: Rice, of course, and perhaps a cool potato or cucumber salad.

WINE: White Riesling or Chenin Blanc. Beer is also good.

Velvet Chicken

THE MANDARIN

Chinese cooks recognize a variety of ways to cook food in oil. The temperature of the pan, the temperature of the oil, and how it is regulated affect the taste and texture of the finished dish, and each nuance is recognized as a separate technique. Velveting, described below, produces a texture quite unlike stir-frying. Follow the procedure carefully.

2 boned whole chicken breasts
1 egg white
1 tablespoon vegetable oil
1 tablespoon cornstarch
1 tablespoon water
½ cup button mushrooms
½ cup fresh snow peas, stems removed
3 cups vegetable oil
½ teaspoon salt
Pinch of sugar
2 or 3 drops sesame oil
1 teaspoon cornstarch dissolved in 1 teaspoon water
1 tablespoon Hsao Shing wine or dry sherry

Slice the chicken as thinly as possible. (It helps to freeze the chicken partially to get the thinnest slices. Ideally, the slices should be translucent.) Put the chicken slices in a bowl with the egg white, 1 tablespoon vegetable oil, 1 tablespoon cornstarch, and the water. Mix them thoroughly.

Put the mushrooms in a strainer and lower them into boiling broth or water to cook them slightly. Drain them well and combine them with the snow peas. Set them aside to cool a bit.

In a wok over high heat, put 2 cups of the oil to heat up. When it is very hot, add 1 cup of cold oil to cool it a bit. Put the chicken in the oil and turn the heat off immediately. Stir the chicken gently in the cooling oil until it turns opaque, then remove it with a strainer and set it aside. Remove all but 2 tablespoons of the oil and turn the heat up again.

When the oil is quite hot, add the mushrooms and pea pods, stir them to coat them with the oil, and add the chicken, salt, sugar, sesame oil, cornstarch, and wine. Stir-fry the food for 30 seconds and serve it immediately.

Makes 2 servings as a main dish by itself, 6 servings in the context of a Chinese meal of several courses.

SERVING SUGGESTION: In the context of a Chinese banquet, this comes after the appetizers but before the really hot or spicy dishes. It is quite delicate, and for contrast many Chinese cooks like to follow it with a robust, spicy dish.

WINE: Chenin Blanc or White Riesling.

Bastilla

MAMOUNIA

A Moroccan cook is judged by the quality of her bastilla, which is rather inelegantly translated as "pigeon pie." The traditional recipe calls for making the dough by hand on a hot plate, which takes exceptional skill. Most Moroccan restaurants are happy to substitute phyllo (or filo) leaves, also known as strudel leaves. Also, instead of expensive squab, most Bastillas today are made with chicken, as is this one.

The Chicken:
1 frying chicken, about 3½ pounds, quartered
1 onion, chopped
1 bunch parsley, chopped
Pinch of salt and pepper
Pinch of coriander (cilantro)
2 tablespoons butter
2 tablespoons oil
Pinch of saffron
4½ cups water

The Almonds:
¼ pound raw or blanched almonds
3 or 4 tablespoons oil

The Sauce:
The liquid from the chicken
5 eggs

The Dough:
1 pound phyllo (filo) pastry (packaged)

For the Bastilla:
2 tablespoons powdered sugar
3 tablespoons powdered cinnamon
Additional butter

Combine all the chicken ingredients in a large skillet with a cover. Simmer the chicken for 1 hour. While the chicken is cooking, fry the almonds in the oil until they are a golden brown. Drain them well in a sieve, then crush them with a mortar and pestle (or in a food processor).

When the chicken is done, remove it from the liquid to cool. Boil down the liquid until all the water evaporates and only the vegetables and the fat are left. Stir in the eggs. Cook them until they form very soft curds, like thin scrambled eggs. Remove the pan from the heat. When the chicken is cool enough to handle, pull it from the bones and cut it into thin strips. Discard the bones.

Lavishly butter an 8-inch skillet. Place a sheet of phyllo dough in the middle of the skillet, then overlap it with additional sheets of dough until the bottom and sides of the skillet are covered and the dough overhangs the edges. Sprinkle the dough with cinnamon, powdered sugar and the crushed almonds. Top this with a layer of phyllo.

Place pieces of shredded chicken on top and then another layer of phyllo. Spread the egg stuffing on top and then another layer of phyllo. Enclose everything, overlapping the bottom "crust" with the top to seal it, forming a sort of pastry tart. Brush the top with butter. Heat the oven to 350°F.

Bake the Bastilla for 10 minutes, or until the top browns nicely. Remove it from the oven and place it over moderate heat for a minute or two to brown the bottom and sides. Slip the bastilla onto a serving plate and dust it with powdered sugar.

Makes 6 servings.

SERVING SUGGESTION: Bastilla is always served as a separate course early in a Moroccan meal, right after the soup and salad.

WINE: A light German or California Riesling.

Arroz con Pollo

SIBONEY

Basically Spanish paella without the seafood, this is a mainstay of Cuban cuisine. Rather sparsely represented in the Bay Area, Cuban food is a happy marriage of Spanish and Caribbean. Marinating the chicken in sour orange (or the combination of citrus given below) is a crucial step that adds the characteristic Cuban touch.

1½ chickens, about 3 pounds each, disjointed
3 cloves garlic, crushed
1 sour orange (Seville orange, or see note)
¼ cup olive oil
1 medium onion, diced
1 medium green pepper, diced
1 small can (4 ounces) tomato sauce
1 tablespoon salt
1½ teaspoons pepper
1 bay leaf
2 cups dry white wine
2 cups chicken broth
Pinch of saffron, crushed
1½ pounds (3¾ cups) uncooked white rice
1 cup cooked peas
1 cup cooked asparagus tips
2 tablespoons chopped pimiento
3 hard-cooked eggs, chopped

Marinate the chicken pieces in the garlic and juice of sour orange for up to 8 hours, refrigerated. (Note: If you cannot obtain sour orange, substitute equal parts lime, grapefruit and sweet orange juice.)

Traditionally, this dish is cooked in a large casserole. It is quite a voluminous dish to serve 6 persons, and a large casserole is necessary. In a pinch, a turkey roaster will do the job.

Heat the oven to 350°F. Drain the chicken and brown it in the olive oil on all sides. Add the onion, pepper, and up to ½ cup of the marinade, including all the garlic. When the vegetables are soft, add the tomato sauce, salt, pepper, bay leaf, and white wine. Stir the chicken broth and saffron together, and add them to the casserole. Cover it, put it in the oven and let it simmer for 30 minutes. Add the rice and continue cooking it, covered, until the rice is soft and has absorbed all the moisture, about 20 minutes longer. Stir in the peas, asparagus tips, pimiento, and egg. Serve one-quarter chicken per serving and plenty of rice.

Makes 6 servings.

SERVING SUGGESTION: This usually serves as a meal in itself, although having lived in South Florida for a number of years and having grown fond of the Cuban restaurants there, I am compelled to top this off with a rich Tocino del Cielo (see Index), and a demitasse of strong espresso.

WINE: Something simple, red or white, like a light Zinfandel or a Chenin Blanc.

Chicken Mattone

FIOR D'ITALIA

For this dish you will need some bricks, or objects of similar size and weight. By cooking the chicken with a weight on it, the excess fat is squeezed out and the chicken comes out with a firm texture.

For Each Serving:
½ frying chicken (from a 2½-pound chicken)
2 tablespoons olive oil
1 teaspoon whole herbs (such as sage, marjoram, oregano, rosemary)
2 cloves garlic, crushed
½ teaspoon salt
Freshly ground pepper
1 tablespoon dry white wine

Heat the oven to 375°F. Brown the chicken skin side down in the oil in a heavy skillet. Turn it skin side up, sprinkle it with the herbs, garlic, salt, and pepper, and place on top of it a brick wrapped in aluminum foil. Put the pan in the oven and let it bake for 25 minutes. (For more than 2 servings, transfer the browned chicken halves to a large baking pan and cover the whole pan with a slightly smaller pan weighted down with bricks or cans.)

When the chicken is done, drain off the fat and add the white wine to the pan. It should sizzle for about 15 seconds. If it doesn't, put the pan over heat briefly to burn off the alcohol in the wine. Serve the chicken with the pan juices spooned on top.

SERVING SUGGESTION: Precede this dish with a serving of potato gnocchi (see Index) and accompany it with a fresh, simply boiled green vegetable.

WINE: A light red, such as Zinfandel, Gamay Noir, Beaujolais or Italian Bardolino.

Duck with Green Peppercorns and Kumquats

FOURNOU'S OVENS

Although this is a bona fide production number, it is also one of the true masterpieces of this collection. Don't let that frighten you off, however. Peeling a kumquat is not difficult; the skin is quite easy to pare with a small paring knife, much easier than an orange or a lemon. Try not to pick up too much of the white pith, and use a chef's knife to julienne-cut the parings. The rest is easy. Green peppercorns are sold in cans in gourmet shops; fresh kumquats are often available in better produce stores and Chinatowns.

The Ducks:
    3 ducks, 4 to 5 pounds each dressed weight
    3 ribs celery, quartered
    3 medium onions, quartered
    3 carrots, cut in chunks
    Salt, pepper

The Sauce:

¼ pound fresh kumquats
2 cups white wine vinegar
½ cup sugar
Juice of 3 large or 4 medium oranges
Juice of 1½ lemons
Pinch of thyme
1 bay leaf
2 cups brown gravy (or, if you have it,
    demi-glace)
½ cup tomato paste
3 ounces green peppercorns
1½ ounces orange-flavored liqueur
Salt, fresh crushed black pepper

Heat the oven to 400°F. Fill the cavities of the ducks with the celery, onions, and carrots. Generously salt and pepper the cavities, tie the ducks with kitchen twine, and place them in a roasting pan on a rack. Roast them for 1½ to 2 hours, continously removing the fat. If they brown too fast, cover them loosely with foil.

Meanwhile, prepare the kumquats. Peel the zest (the orange part of the skin) of all but 6 of the kumquats. Julienne-cut the zest. Grind the peeled kumquats into pulp and juice.

In a 2½- to 3-quart saucepan, cook the vinegar and sugar over high heat until the sugar caramelizes (turns brown). Immediately add the orange and lemon juice and the kumquat pulp. Reduce the heat slightly, then add the thyme, bay leaf, and a pinch of crushed black pepper. Continue to cook until the mixture turns a golden brown. Add the brown gravy and the tomato paste, bring the sauce to a simmer, and let it cook 1 hour. Strain the sauce through a fine sieve.

When the ducks are finished, cut them in half lengthwise and let them drain on a rack while you finish the sauce. Put the strained sauce in a clean saucepan and add the orange liqueur and the green peppercorns. Heat the sauce just to the simmer. Add the julienne-cut kumquat zest. Taste for seasoning. Arrange the ducks on a serving platter. Glaze each duck with a tablespoon of the sauce. Garnish them with the remaining kumquats, thinly sliced. Serve the remaining sauce on the side in a sauceboat.

Makes 6 servings.

SERVING SUGGESTION: Accompany the duck with some fried or sautéed potatoes, or a combination of mashed potatoes, turnips and parsnips lavishly buttered.

WINE: The sweet-sour nature of the sauce requires a young, robust, fruity red wine such as a Beaujolais or a young Zinfandel.

Duck with Olives

RENÉ VERDON'S LE TRIANON

René Verdon's recipe calls for two bottles of Clos de Vougeot, which would make this dish too expensive for 99 percent of us. It works just fine, thank you, with an anonymous Burgundy or Pinot Noir, but since the wine is going to be reduced and its flavor intensified, don't use anything you wouldn't love to drink.

The Ducks:
3 ducks, about 4 pounds each dressed weight
Salt, pepper

The Sauce:
2 medium carrots, sliced
1 medium onion, sliced
2 ribs celery, sliced
1 large shallot, finely chopped
2 cloves garlic, finely chopped
2 tablespoons chopped parsley
2 bay leaves
½ teaspoon thyme
2 tablespoons flour
2 bottles (or 1 magnum) dry red wine, preferably Burgundy or Pinot Noir
2 cups chicken broth

The Final Braising:
1½ tablespoons butter
½ cup brandy
½ pound mushrooms, quartered
1 cup green olives
3 tablespoons cornstarch dissolved in 2 tablespoons water

Heat the oven to 350°F. Season the inside of the ducks with salt and pepper. Put the ducks on a rack in a roasting pan, breast up. Roast them without basting for one hour. This is to melt some of the fat off the duck. Reserve the fat. When the duck is cool enough to handle, cut it into serving pieces. Remove the skin.

In a large skillet, heat the reserved fat from the roasting pan. In it, brown the gizzard, heart, neck and miscellaneous scraps of the duck along with the carrots, onion, celery, shallot, garlic, and parsley. When everything is golden brown, pour off all the fat you can. Add the bay leaves, thyme, flour, red wine and broth. Turn up the heat and let it reduce by half.

In another skillet, heat the butter and lightly brown the cut-up duck. Pour the brandy over the duck and ignite it, taking care to avert your face first. When the flames die away, strain the sauce over the duck, add the mushrooms and olives, cover the pan, and simmer it gently for 1 hour, or until the duck is tender.

(If you do not have a skillet large enough to accommodate the duck, follow this alternate method: Heat the oven to 325°F. Brown the duck in the butter in the largest skillet you have, but do not crowd the skillet. Do this in two or three shifts. Flame the duck with the appropriate portion of brandy and transfer it to a large casserole, or two smaller ones. Strain the sauce over the duck and add the mushrooms and olives, or portion the mushrooms and olives between the casseroles if you use more than one. Cover the casseroles and bake the duck for 1 hour, or until it is tender.)

Stir the cornstarch into the simmering sauce to thicken it. The reserved duck skin can be sautéed crisp and used to garnish the duck.

Makes 6 servings.

SERVING SUGGESTION: Rice or noodles to catch the sauce, of course, and a green vegetable.

WINE: Red Burgundy or Pinot Noir.

Whole Grilled Duck

CHEZ PANISSE

For the barbecue grill, a marinated whole duck is a far classier act than your basic sirloin steak. A little melted butter drizzled over the top is all the sauce it needs. The key is the fresh herbs, which add the subtlty that lifts the duck out of the ordinary.

For Each 4-pound Duck:
2 carrots, thinly sliced

1 medium onion, thinly sliced
Several branches of fresh herbs—thyme, rosemary,
    oregano, tarragon
Red wine

Slice the duck down the backbone and flatten it with your hands. You may have to lean hard on the duck to do it, but it must lie flat. Scatter half the carrots, onion, and herbs in the bottom of a pan large enough to hold the duck(s). The pan should be ceramic or stainless steel; aluminum will react with the wine to add a metallic taste and odd color. Cover the duck(s) with the remaining carrots, onion, and herbs and pour on enough red wine to cover them. Let them marinate at room temperature for several hours.

Heat the oven to 450°F. Remove the duck(s) from the marinade. Put them on a rack in a roasting pan. Put them in the preheated oven for 30 minutes to render the fat. Then finish cooking them over smoky hot charcoal, mostly on the skin side, until they are done, about 30 to 40 minutes. Timing depends on the heat of the charcoal and the distance from the heat.

Makes 2 to 4 servings.

SERVING SUGGESTION: The classic accompaniment is fried shoestring potatoes, although a baked potato stuffed with mushrooms is easier to handle and equally delicious.

WINE: A Cabernet Sauvignon with at least 6 or 7 years' age, or a Bordeaux.

NOTE: The duck can be prepared up to the point of rendering the fat. After it has been in the oven for 30 minutes, it can be kept at room temperature for several hours before being finished over charcoal. Test the duck for doneness by cutting into it at the thickest point.

Pi Pa Duck

EMPRESS OF CHINA

The *pi pa* is a Chinese stringed instrument like the guitar. Its connection with duck is explained by a legend that goes back to the Han Dynasty (about 200 B.C.). To appease the Mongols, who were making ready to plunder the Han Court, the emperor sent the Mongol leader a beautiful maiden for marriage. The maiden, Lady Huang Chao Jiun, considered one of the four greatest beauties in Chinese history, was a great musician whose instrument was the *pi pa*. This is reputedly her favorite dish.

1 duck, 4 to 5 pounds
1 cup bottled brown bean sauce
1 cup red bean curd
1 tablespoon Hsao Shing wine or dry sherry
1 teaspoon sugar
2 scallions, finely chopped
3 quarter-size slices fresh ginger root, finely chopped
¼ cup honey

Rinse the duck and pat it dry. Mix the brown bean sauce, red bean curd, wine, sugar, scallions, and ginger root to make a marinating paste. Brush the marinade generously inside the duck. Wrap the duck in plastic wrap or toweling and refrigerate it for at least 1 hour. Hang the duck in a cool place for 3 to 4 hours. This step can be omitted, but it helps to make the skin properly crisp. If you omit this step, use several paper towels to dry the skin thoroughly.

Heat the oven to 400°F. Paint the duck with honey. Place it on a rack, on a vertical roaster rack, or hang it from the top shelf of the oven. Roast it for 1 hour, 45 minutes, or until the skin is crispy and the duck is cooked through. Hack the duck into bite-size pieces with a cleaver or a heavy chef's knife. Arrange the pieces on a serving platter.

Makes 6 servings, or 3 servings as a main course.

SERVING SUGGESTION: In a Chinese meal, this is served as a separate course. It could be accompanied by mixed vegetables stir-fried in a simple sauce.

WINE: A young, fruity Beaujolais or Zinfandel.

Duckling with Turnips

LA BOURGOGNE

Duck and turnips is a classic combination in French cuisine, but American restaurants seem to have difficulty progressing beyond duck with orange sauce. In this case, the turnips add their flavor without dominating the dish.

For 2 Servings:

1 duck, 4 to 5 pounds
4 tablespoons butter (preferably clarified), divided
2 large turnips
½ pound small white onions
2 tablespoons confectioners' sugar, divided
1 cup dry white wine
1½ cups veal stock or chicken broth
Salt, pepper
Bouquet garni (bay leaf, thyme, parsley and ½ rib celery tied in a little bundle)

Heat the oven to 350°F.
In a skillet, brown the duck in half the butter on all sides. Put it in a casserole just large enough to hold it. Cover the casserole and bake it for 30 minutes.

Meanwhile, peel and quarter the turnips, then trim them into olive shapes. Peel the white onions. Sauté the turnips in 1 tablespoon of the remaining butter with 1 tablespoon of the powdered sugar. Cook them until they are nicely glazed, then set them aside. Repeat the process with the onions. After the duck has cooked 30 minutes, pour off the fat and add the vegetables to the casserole along with the wine, broth, a sprinkling of salt and pepper, and the bouquet garni. Cover the casserole and bake it 1 hour, or until the duck is done (test by wiggling a leg; it should move freely in its socket).

When the duck is done, remove the vegetables and the duck to a platter. Serve it as is, or make a sauce from the juices in the pot by stirring a little of the warm juices into 2 tablespoons cornstarch, then stirring the cornstarch paste into the sauce. Let it boil until it acquires a bit of a sheen, about 2 minutes. Serve the sauce separately, or poured over the duck.

SERVING SUGGESTION: Rice or noodles to catch the sauce, and follow with a crisp salad.

WINE: A young Cabernet Sauvignon, Merlot, or St. Émilion.

Stuffed Squab or Cornish Hen with Black Cherry Sauce

COW HOLLOW INN

Don't worry. It's not too sweet. The couscous filling is exciting and different. The combination is striking. Fresh cherries make a big difference, in season.

The Squabs:
6 squabs or Cornish hens, 1 to 1¼ pounds each

The Stuffing:
8 scallions, finely chopped
2 ribs celery, finely chopped
1 cup (2 sticks) butter
2 teaspoons each: sage, chervil, thyme
2 teaspoons salt
½ teaspoon pepper
2 cups chicken broth
1 cup uncooked couscous
Squab livers, chopped
8 ounces ground veal

The Sauce:
4 dozen dark sweet cherries, halved and pitted
2 cups water
2 cups Port wine
3 tablespoons Kirsch
2 tablespoons cornstarch
Pinch of ground allspice

Rinse and pat dry the squabs. Season them inside and out lightly with salt and pepper. Heat the oven to 350°F.

In a large skillet, sauté the scallions and the celery in the butter until they are soft. Add the herbs, salt, pepper, and broth. Bring it to a boil. Add the couscous in a thin stream (to keep it from lumping), bring it to a boil, and remove the pan from the heat. Cover it tightly and let it sit for 10 to 15 minutes, or until the liquid is totally absorbed.

Meanwhile, in another pan, sauté the livers and the veal until they are browned (If the veal is not fat enough to provide its own sautéing medium, add a little oil or butter).

Stuff the birds with the couscous and veal mixture. Put them on a rack in a roasting pan and roast them for 1½ hours, or until they are cooked through.

Meanwhile, make the sauce. Plump the cherries in the water and the Port for 10 minutes. (If fresh cherries are not available, use frozen or canned.) Put the cherries and wine in a saucepan and simmer them for 20 minutes, or until the cherries are quite soft. Add ¼ cup of the pan juices and purée the sauce in a blender, food processor, or food mill. Strain it into a clean saucepan and bring it to a boil. Use the Kirsch to moisten the cornstarch and stir it into the sauce along with the allspice.

When the birds are done, glaze them lightly with the sauce and pass the rest in a sauceboat. Garnish them with additional fresh or canned cherries.

Makes 6 servings.

SERVING SUGGESTION: A green vegetable is all this needs to be a complete course. Precede it with a light soup and follow with a crisp salad.

WINE: A big, fruity Zinfandel or Cabernet Sauvignon.

Braised Squab

FOUR SEASONS-CLIFT HOTEL

As expensive as squabs are, they deserve lavish treatment. A sauce rich with the flavors of mushrooms, Port wine, garlic, coriander, and red currant jelly stands up nobly to the bird's own assertive flavors. As a braised dish, most of the preparation attention comes an hour before you serve it, so it does not require a great deal of last-minute work.

The Squabs:
    6 squabs, about 1 pound each
    6 slices lemon
    6 slices onion
    Thyme
    Sage
    6 teaspoons red currant jelly
    Salt, pepper

Flour
4 tablespoons butter

The Braising Liquid:

4 tablespoons butter
1 rib celery, diced
1 medium onion, diced
1 carrot, diced
½ cup finely chopped mushroom stems (or whole mushrooms)
3 tablespoons finely chopped parsley stems (or whole parsley)
2 bay leaves
½ teaspoon peppercorns
1 teaspoon juniper berries
½ branch fresh thyme (or pinch of dried)
½ teaspoon dried sage
3 cloves garlic, peeled and crushed
½ teaspoon coriander seed
1¾ cups Port wine
2 cups beef broth or brown stock
2 cups brown gravy (or, if you have it, demi-glace sauce)
¼ cup red currant jelly

Stuff each squab with a lemon slice and an onion slice, a pinch each of thyme and sage, and a teaspoon of currant jelly. Season it with salt and pepper and dredge it in flour. Heat the 4 tablespoons butter in a large sauté pan and brown the birds all over. Set them aside.

In the remaining 4 tablespoons butter, lightly brown the celery, onion, carrot, mushroom, and parsley. Add the remaining ingredients except the currant jelly. (If it all won't fit in the same pan, just add the wine.) If the pan is big enough to accommodate the braising liquid and the squabs, simply add the squabs to the pan breast down, cover them and braise them over gentle heat for 1 hour. If the pan is not large enough, arrange the squabs breast down in a deep baking pan (even a turkey roaster) and pour the braising liquid over them. Cover the pan and bake the squabs for 1 hour at 350°F.

When the squabs are done, keep them warm while you strain the sauce into a saucepan and bring it to a boil, reducing it until it thickens to light sauce, just thick enough to coat the spoon. Stir in the currant jelly and glaze the birds with the sauce.

Makes 6 servings.

SERVING SUGGESTION: At the Four Seasons-Clift's French Room, this is served on a fried crouton and garnished with a poached apple cut in half crosswise, the hollowed core filled with currant jelly.

WINE: Dig through the cellar for that superb 10-year-old Cabernet Sauvignon or classified-growth Médoc you've been saving for a special occasion.

Minced Squab

THE MANDARIN

The best Chinese cooks strive to cut all the vegetables into tiny dice precisely the same size. Using a food processor speeds the process and it comes out tasting just as good, but the dish loses some of its elegance. Strike your own balance. If you go to the trouble of mincing all the vegetables carefully, go the final step and trim the lettuce leaves so they are all the same size and shape.

2 large squabs (over 1 pound each)
1 dozen Chinese black mushrooms, soaked in warm water
1 quarter-size ginger root
1 cup water chestnuts
1 slice (about 3 inches square) country ham
2 scallions, white part only
¼ cup vegetable oil
1 tablespoon Hsao Shing wine or dry sherry
Pinch of white pepper
1 tablespoon bottled oyster sauce
1 tablespoon thin soy sauce
½ teaspoon sugar
½ teaspoon sesame oil
1 tablespoon cornstarch dissolved in 2 teaspoons water
12 leaves iceberg lettuce (preferably from a loosely packed head)

Bone and finely chop the squab meat. Drain, squeeze dry, and finely chop the mushrooms. Peel and smash the ginger. Finely chop the water chestnuts. (The squab, mushrooms and water chestnuts should be cut in tiny pieces as close to the same size as possible; the quantities should be in the proportions 4 parts squab to 3 parts each mushrooms and water chestnuts.) Finely chop the ham, enough to make 3 tablespoons. Finally, finely chop the scallions.

Heat the oil over a high flame in a wok, moistening the sides of the pan with it. Add the squab meat and stir-fry it until it separates into small pieces, about 20 seconds. Add the mushrooms, ginger, water chestnuts, and ham. Stir-fry them until they are well mixed. Add the Hsao Shing, pepper, oyster sauce, soy, sugar, and sesame oil. Stir-fry them briefly to blend them into the mixture. Stir in the cornstarch solution and turn off the heat. Serve the minced squab with a separate plate of lettuce leaves.

To eat the minced squab, spoon a couple of tablespoons of the filling into a lettuce leaf and roll it up like a burrito or an egg roll. Eat it with your hands.

Makes 6 servings as a first course.

SERVING SUGGESTION: In the context of a Chinese banquet, this comes at the end of the appetizer sequence. As one of the great dishes in Chinese cuisine, it deserves a place of its own in any meal. It should not be served with anything else.

WINE: Zinfandel or Gamay Beaujolais.

Meat

Roast Sirloin in a Salt Coat

PINEBROOK INN

This is a special-occasion project, but one well worth doing for a gathering of a dozen guests, give or take a few. The cut of meat called for is one of the finest on the animal, the other side of the T-bone from the tenderloin. It makes a superb roast, and this method locks in the juices and seals in the flavor. It also makes a dramatic presentation when you crack the crust to reveal a beautifully juicy roast.

1 boneless strip loin of beef, 10 to 12 pounds
2 teaspoons freshly ground pepper
½ teaspoon granulated garlic powder
¼ cup oil
4 pounds plain table salt
3 pounds rock salt
1 pound cornstarch
4 egg whites
2 teaspoons ground thyme
1½ cups water
1 medium onion, quartered
½ medium carrot, cut in chunks
½ medium leek, cut in 1-inch pieces
1 rib celery, cut in 1-inch pieces
4 cups cold water

Request a top-quality U.S. Prime strip loin from your butcher. Trim any excess fat and rub the pepper and garlic into the meat. Heat the oven to 450°F. Put the oil in a roasting pan in the oven while it heats up. When the oil is quite hot, put the roast in the pan and bake it for 15 minutes, then turn the meat and bake it for 15 minutes longer. This is to brown the meat. Remove it from the oven and lower the heat to 400°F. Let the meat cool while you mix the coating.

Combine the salts, cornstarch, egg whites, thyme, and water in a large mixing bowl to make a paste. Smear this ½-inch thick over the meat and return it to the roasting pan. Roast it 45 minutes for rare, 1 hour for medium, 1 hour 15 minutes for well done. Remove the meat from the pan and add the remaining ingredients.

On top of the stove, bring the juices to a boil, then lower the heat to a simmer. Skim off as much of the fat as you can and let the juices cook for 10 minutes with the vegetables. Strain the juices and serve them with the meat.

To serve the roast, which by now will be encased in a rock–hard coating, crack the coating with a hammer. Do this in front of your guests for best effect. The coating will then peel off in great chunks. Cut the meat into ½-inch slices and serve it with a gravy boat of the strained juices.

Makes 12 servings.

SERVING SUGGESTION: Accompany this with a baked potato and sliced mushrooms sautéed with a green vegetable such as Brussels sprouts or zucchini.

WINE: A fine Pinot Noir or a great Burgundy will do this justice.

Beef Vinaigrette

GOLDEN EAGLE

A spicy vinaigrette makes a lovely sauce for *hot* pot roast, an unusual combination that has become one of critic Robert Finigan's favorites at the Golden Eagle.

The Beef:

1 beef brisket, about 6 pounds
1 onion, halved
1 clove garlic, peeled
1 carrot, halved lengthwise
2 ribs celery
2 bay leaves
1 teaspoon salt
Golden Eagle Sauce Vinaigrette (see recipe below)

Heat the oven to 325°F. Trim as much surface fat as possible from the beef. Put it in a baking pan large enough to accommodate it. Surround it with the vegetables and sprinkle it with the salt. Pour in enough water to cover it. Cover the pan and bake it for 2 to 2½ hours, or until the brisket is tender. Drain the beef. Slice it thinly and arrange the slices on a serving platter. While the beef is still hot, cover it with the Sauce Vinaigrette.

The Sauce Vinaigrette:

1 cup vegetable oil
1 cup olive oil
1 cup mild white wine vinegar
¼ cup finely chopped red onions

2 tablespoons finely chopped shallots
¼ cup finely chopped parsley
2 tablespoons finely chopped chives
3 tablespoons chopped pimiento
¼ cup chopped capers
2 teaspoons white pepper
2 teaspoons salt
1 tablespoon dry mustard
2 teaspoons garlic powder (not garlic salt)
3 dashes Tabasco sauce
6 hard-cooked eggs, chopped

Beat the oils and the vinegar together until they are smooth. Stir in the remaining ingredients.

Makes 12 servings.

SERVING SUGGESTION: Simple green vegetables such as broccoli or zucchini, and perhaps a bit of sautéed carrots complement this hearty, homey dish.

WINE: Choose a red wine with lively acid balance, such as an Italian Bardolino or Spanish Rioja.

Sauerbraten

SCHROEDER'S

This traditional German dish gets a classic treatment from Schroeder's, which does not go in for the addition of crumbled ginger snaps popular with so many cooks. The spicy flavors come from the whole spices added to the marinade and, later, to the sauce.

5 pounds beef top round or rump, in one piece
2 cups vinegar
4 cups water
1 large onion, sliced
¼ cup whole mixed spices (cloves, pepper, allspice, cinnamon)
1 teaspoon salt
2 tablespoons shortening
3 tablespoons flour
½ cup water
½ cup red wine (or more)
2 tablespoons sugar

Put the beef in a glass or ceramic bowl deep enough to hold the 6 cups of liquid, onion, and spices. Pour the vinegar, water, onion, mixed spices, and salt over the meat and let it marinate for 2 to 3 days, refrigerated, turning it frequently.

Heat the oven to 350°F. In a small saucepan, melt the shortening, then add the flour to make a roux. When the raw-flour aroma dissipates, add the water and ½ cup red wine. Stir in the sugar. When the mixture thickens and boils, remove it from the heat. Drain the meat and place it in a roasting pan. Combine the spices from the marinade with the wine sauce and pour it over the meat. Bake the meat in the oven for 2½ to 3 hours, turning and basting it frequently. Continue to bake until it is tender.

When the meat is done, strain the pan juices. Thicken them, if necessary, with a little cornstarch or arrowroot. If the sauce is not sour enough, add a bit more vinegar to taste.

Makes 6 servings.

SERVING SUGGESTION: Accompany the meat with freshly fried Potato Pancakes and Red Cabbage German Style (see index for both).

WINE: Beer does not compete with the vinegar and sugar.

Rindsrouladen

BEETHOVEN

Have the butcher pound the beef slices as thin as possible for these hearty German beef rollmops, otherwise they can be difficult to roll tightly and neatly.

The Rouladen:
3 medium onions, halved and thinly sliced
4 tablespoons vegetable oil
12 thin slices beef top round, about 3 ounces each
Salt, pepper
4 tablespoons (approximately) German mustard
6 slices bacon, cut in half
12 slices kosher dill pickles

The Braising Liquid and Sauce:
2 onions, thinly sliced
2 ribs celery, thinly sliced

2 carrots, thinly sliced
2 cloves garlic, finely chopped
3 tablespoons oil
1 small can (6 ounces) tomato paste
2 cups dry red wine
2 bay leaves
1 teaspoon dried rosemary (or ½ teaspoon fresh)
1 teaspoon dried thyme (or ½ teaspoon fresh)
1 teaspoon salt
¼ teaspoon pepper
Dash of Worcestershire sauce

Brown the halved and sliced onions in the oil and set them aside.

Pound the beef slices paper thin. Lightly salt and pepper each one, spread them with 1 teaspoon each mustard and some of the sautéed onions. Place ½ slice of bacon on each one, and a slice of pickle. Roll up the slices. Mold each together with a wooden toothpick. Brown the Rouladen in a little vegetable oil. Set them aside.

For the braising liquid, in a large saucepan or stew pot, brown the onions, celery, carrots, and garlic in the oil. Add the tomato paste, wine, and remaining seasonings, stir them well, and add the Rouladen. Simmer the Rouladen in the sauce for 1 hour 15 minutes. Remove the Rouladen to a serving platter. Strain the sauce and pour it over the Rouladen.

Makes 6 servings.

SERVING SUGGESTION: Baked or boiled potato and some bread to sop up the sauce are mandatory.

WINE: A young, rich Zinfandel or Gamay works all right, but beer works better.

Nalesniki

WARSZAWA

Serve these crêpes with plenty of sour cream as a kind of sauce. The filling is quite crumbly, and the sour cream holds it together nicely.

The Crêpes:
2 large eggs
½ cup milk

½ cup water
Dash of salt
Pinch of pepper
2 tablespoons butter, melted
⅔ cup flour

The Filling:

1½ pounds lean ground beef
½ pound Polish sausage, skinned and crumbled
1 ounce imported dried mushrooms (or ½ pound
    fresh), soaked, squeezed dry, and chopped
1 medium onion, finely chopped
¼ cup butter
Salt, pepper

For the Pan:

¼ cup (or more) butter, melted

In a 4-cup measure or a mixing bowl, beat the eggs with the milk and water until they are smooth. Add the remaining crêpe ingredients and beat them until they are smooth. Let this mixture stand for 30 minutes.

Grease a 6- or 7-inch skillet with a little butter. Put it over moderate heat. Give it several minutes to heat up thoroughly, then pour in 2 tablespoons of the batter, tilting the pan to distribute it evenly. Let the crêpe cook for 30 seconds, or until it browns lightly (check by lifting at the edge). Turn the crêpe to lightly brown the other side. Stack the crêpes, separated by sheets of wax paper. This should make a dozen crêpes.

In a large skillet, brown the ground beef and crumbled Polish sausage in their own fat. Drain the fat and add the mushrooms, onion, and butter. Cook over moderate heat until the onion softens. Season the mixture to taste with salt and pepper. Let the mixture cool.

Heat the oven to 350°F. In a baking pan large enough to hold a dozen crêpes, brush the bottom and sides with about 1 tablespoon of the melted butter. Divide the filling among the 12 crêpes, roll them, and arrange them in the baking pan. Pour the remaining butter over the crêpes and bake them for 20 minutes, or until they brown appetizingly. Serve them with sour cream for a garnish.

Makes 6 servings.

SERVING SUGGESTION: Make a Polish meal; start with some borscht (see Index) and conclude with the Walnut Torte (see Index).

WINE: Any hearty red wine. A fresh Zinfandel is especially nice.

Braised Oxtails

ORIGINAL JOE'S

For some reason, Saturday has become the day a number of San Francisco restaurants offer braised oxtails as a daily special. The cooking time is long, but it takes that long to get those tough little rascals tender enough to cut with a fork. Joe's has figured out how to do it and retain all that rich, meaty flavor.

6 pounds oxtails, disjointed
¼ cup olive oil
2 teaspoons salt
4 or 5 grindings of pepper
Pinch of nutmeg
Pinch of mace
Pinch of paprika
2 or 3 cloves garlic, peeled and finely chopped
1 cup white wine
1 small onion, chopped
½ rib celery, chopped
1 medium carrot, chopped
½ small green pepper, chopped
2 tablespoons butter
4 cups beef broth
½ cup dry vermouth

Heat the oven to 375°F. Toss the oxtails in the olive oil to coat them well. Arrange them in a large roasting pan in one layer. Put them in the oven to brown on all sides, turning them after 30 minutes. It should take about 1 hour to 1½ hours for them to brown nicely. Sprinkle the oxtails with salt, pepper, nutmeg, mace, paprika, garlic, and white wine. Return them to the oven. Reduce the heat to 325°F. and let them bake an additional 30 to 60 minutes, depending on how long the original browning took. To this point, the cooking time should be 2 hours. Drain the oxtails.

In a skillet, sauté the onion, celery, carrot, and green pepper in the butter until the vegetables are soft. Pour this over the oxtails along with the beef broth and the vermouth. Cover the pan and bake them at least 2 more hours, or until they are tender. Serve them with some of the sauce that forms in the pan.

Makes 6 servings.

SERVING SUGGESTION: Rice to catch the sauce and mixed vegetables (peas, carrots, corn, zucchini, spinach).

WINE: A rich Côte de Rhône, Chateaneuf-du-Pape or Petite Sirah.

Sweetbreads Trader Vic's Style

TRADER VIC'S

Sweetbreads sautéed in butter and served with a simple pan sauce spiked with, of all things, Worcestershire sauce and shallots is not exactly typical fare, but it's the kind of thing a creative mind like Vic Bergeron turns out routinely.

For 2 or 3 Servings:
1 pound sweetbreads
Vinegar
Salt
Lemon Juice

Flour
3 to 4 tablespoons butter
½ cup finely chopped shallots
¼ pound fresh button mushrooms (or 1 small can, 2 ounces, drained)
½ cup dry white wine
2 tablespoons chicken broth
1 teaspoon Worcestershire sauce
Salt and freshly ground pepper
Finely chopped parsley

Soak the sweetbreads in several changes of cold water for 2 hours. Then soak them 1 hour longer in cold water to which 1 tablespoon of vinegar has been added for each quart. Gently pull off as much of the outer membrane as possible without tearing the sweetbreads. Trim off any tubes or discolored portions. Put the sweetbreads in a large saucepan with 1 quart of water, 1 teaspoon of salt and 1 teaspoon of lemon juice or vinegar. Simmer them, uncovered, for 15 minutes. Drain them, plunge them into ice water, and let them stand for 5 minutes. Drain them well and dry them on paper towels. All this can be done well in advance.

Cut the sweetbreads into pieces no larger than ¾ inch. Dust them with the flour. In a large, heavy frying pan over medium-high heat, melt the butter and brown the sweetbreads. Add the shallots and toss them briefly with the sweetbreads. Add the mushrooms, wine, broth, and Worcestershire. Continue cooking until the liquid reduces to a thin sauce that cloaks the sweetbreads. Season the dish generously with salt and pepper, and sprinkle it lightly with parsley.

Makes 3 home servings, 2 of restaurant size.

SERVING SUGGESTION: A little rice to catch the sauce and a fresh vegetable make this a lovely luncheon or late supper.

WINE: Pinot Noir makes a perfect combination with the meaty flavor of the sweetbreads.

NOTE: Unless you have a restaurant stove, this dish is impractical to make for more than 3 or 4 servings at home, since you cannot fit more than a pound of sweetbreads comfortably into a frying pan that will fit on a home stove.

Tripe à la Béarnaise

DÉLICES DE FRANCE

The reason for the calves' feet is to add plenty of gelatinous texture to the mixture, because the dish is served cold, sliced and with plenty of spicy mustard. Kosher butchers are the best source of calves' feet, although you may have to settle for beef feet. There isn't much meat on them, but they add muscular texture and richness.

2½ pounds beef tripe
½ pound pork rind
¼ pound salt pork
3 carrots (¼ pound), diced (½ inch)
1 medium onion, diced
1 large or 2 medium tomatoes, diced
1 medium to large leek, diced (white part only)
¼ cup white wine
1 pound, 12 ounces calves' feet or beef feet
1 tablespoon salt
½ teaspoon each: pepper, garlic, thyme
1 bay leaf
2 cloves

Pinch of cayenne
1 tablespoon brandy
4 cups beef broth

Cut the tripe into ½-inch squares. Put it in a large pot and cover it with water. Bring it to a boil. Let it boil 5 minutes, then pour off the water and rinse the tripe.

Meanwhile, cut the pork rind and salt pork into ½-inch pieces. Rinse out the saucepan and render the salt pork gently over low heat. When it has released its fat, add the tripe, pork rind, carrot, onion, tomato, and leek. Brown them, stirring frequently, then add the white wine, the calves' feet, and all the remaining ingredients. If the beef broth is not enough to cover everything with liquid, add enough water to do so. Cover the pot and let it simmer very gently for 10 to 12 hours. Pour it into a mold and chill it. Serve it in generous slices.

Makes 15 to 18 servings.

SERVING SUGGESTION: With a few other delicatessen meats, this makes a terrific cornerstone for an assorted cold plate of meats and patés the French call "assiettes." Spicy mustard is de rigueur.

WINE: A full-bodied Sauvignon Blanc or Gewurztraminer.

Veal Stelvio

FIOR D'ITALIA

Once the ingredients are together, it only takes 5 minutes to produce this for 2 persons, making it an ideal dish for a special dinner after a busy day.

For Each Serving:
3 thin slices veal (scaloppine), pounded thin
Flour
2 tablespoons butter
1 tablespoon oil
3 fresh mushrooms, sliced
2 slices prosciutto, julienne-cut
3 tablespoons dry white wine
½ teaspoon finely chopped shallots
½ teaspoon finely chopped garlic
Salt, pepper
2 tablespoons butter, softened

No more than 5 minutes before you are ready to serve, dredge the veal in the flour. Shake the slices to remove any excess flour. Heat the butter and oil in a skillet over a fairly high flame. When the fat is quite hot, brown the veal quickly—not more than 30 seconds on each side. Remove the veal with tongs and reserve it. Sauté the mushrooms and the prosciutto in the fat remaining in the skillet. After 30 seconds, pour off any excess fat and add the wine, shallots, and garlic. After another 30 seconds, reduce the heat and return the slices of veal to the pan.

Turn the veal to coat it with the sauce, sprinkling it lightly with salt and pepper. Swirl in the 2 tablespoons of softened butter and turn the veal and its sauce out onto a serving plate.

SERVING SUGGESTION: Broccoli, asparagus, or green beans quickly boiled and served slightly crisp.

WINE: A rich red wine such as Chianti Classico, Ghemme, Gattinara or Barbera.

NOTE: This is one of those restaurant-style dishes that works admirably for 1 or 2 persons, but gets to be something of a chore for 6. With a large enough skillet, you can get away with producing the dish in batches of 3 servings.

Veal Scaloppine alla Doros

DOROS

The difficult part of this recipe is coordinating the sautéing of the eggplants, the mushrooms, and finally the veal so they come out together. I solve the problem by baking the eggplants in a hot oven, first brushing them lavishly with butter. Meanwhile the mushrooms can be sautéed in one pan, the veal at the last minute in another. The effort is worth it.

18 slices (¼ inch thick) eggplant (2 eggplants)
½ cup butter, melted
1½ pounds mushrooms, sliced
1 cup butter
18 thin slices veal (scaloppine), pounded flat
Flour, seasoned with salt and pepper
⅓ cup dry white wine
¾ cup brown gravy (or demi-glace, if you have it)

1½ tablespoons chopped shallot
3 tablespoons softened butter
2 tablespoons fresh chopped parsley

Heat the oven to 400°F. Arrange the eggplant slices on a baking sheet. Brush them with half the ½ cup melted butter. Bake them for 5 minutes, turn them, brush the other side with melted butter, and bake 5 minutes longer.

While the eggplant is baking, sauté the mushrooms in ½ cup butter in a large skillet. Dredge the veal in seasoned flour, shake off the excess, and sauté the slices quickly in the remaining ½ cup butter. They only need about 30 seconds on each side, just long enough to brown lightly. As the veal is browned, alternate overlapping slices of veal and eggplant on a bed of mushrooms.

Pour off the butter from the veal pan and quickly add the wine, the gravy, and the shallots. Simmer for 3 minutes. Swirl in the 3 tablespoons softened butter, pour the sauce over the veal and eggplant slices, and sprinkle the surface with parsley.

Makes 6 servings.

SERVING SUGGESTION: Use the Stuffed Tomatoes alla Medici (see Index), as a combination vegetable and garnish.

WINE: A light Italian red such a Valpolicella, or a light California Zinfandel or Gamay.

NOTE: This is one of those recipes that works best in smaller quantities—2 or 3 servings. Just divide the quantities in the recipes in half for 3 servings, by three for 2 servings.

Le Veau de Pêcheur

LA MÈRE DUQUESNE

A Busby Berkeley production number of veal dishes, this multi-stage extravaganza offers a wide palette of color, texture, and flavor in a single dish. It takes a lot of preparation, but once everything is ready it goes together quickly.

The Seafoods:
1 cup dry white wine
2 shallots, chopped
1 bay leaf
½ pound scallops (cut in half if they are large)
¼ pound medium prawns (shrimp)
¼ cup bay shrimp
½ pound mushrooms, thickly sliced

The Sauce:
¼ cup flour
¼ cup butter
2 cups half-and-half

The Spinach:
1½ cups milk
1 chicken bouillon cube
1 pound fresh spinach, chopped, or 1 package (10 ounces) frozen spinach
Pinch of nutmeg
Salt, pepper to taste

The Veal:
6 large veal scallops
Flour

2 tablespoons butter
2 tablespoons oil

Put the wine, shallots, and bay leaf in a saucepan. Bring it to a boil. Add the scallops, prawns, shrimp, and mushrooms. When the liquid boils, reduce the heat and let it simmer until the seafood has turned opaque. Drain the seafood, but reserve the liquid.

In another saucepan, combine the flour and the butter and cook it, stirring with a wire whisk, until it forms a roux, about 2 minutes. Add the strained poaching liquid and the cream. Continue to cook, stirring, until the mixture thickens. Let it simmer for 15 minutes.

Heat the milk in a skillet or a saucepan. Dissolve the bouillon cube in it. Bring it to a boil and reduce the volume by one-third, then add the spinach (thawed and drained if using frozen) and the nutmeg. Boil it until the spinach is done, 3 to 5 minutes. Thicken the mixture with some additional roux, or with 1 tablespoon cornstarch dissolved in 2 teaspoons water. Season it to taste with salt and pepper. Keep it warm. Just before you sauté the veal, stir the seafoods into the cream sauce. Do not let it boil.

Dip the veal scallops in flour. Shake off any excess flour. Sprinkle them with salt and pepper. Over high heat, melt the butter with the oil in a large skillet. When the foam subsides, sauté the veal for 1 to 1½ minutes on each side (depending on its thickness).

While the veal is sautéing, make 6 piles of spinach on individual plates. Flatten the mounds of spinach. When the veal is cooked, lay one slice on each pile of spinach. Spoon on the seafood sauce.

Makes 6 servings.

SERVING SUGGESTION: It's complete in itself as a single course, although a few crisp fried potatoes make an interesting side dish contrast.

WINE: A full-bodied Sauvignon Blanc or Chardonnay.

Veal Cardinal

SARDINE FACTORY

Veal, lobster tails (or jumbo prawns), and mushrooms in a simple pan sauce of white wine, lemon juice, garlic, and butter—expensive, luxurious ingredients simply prepared. Brown the veal scallops in shifts so as not to crowd the pan (and hinder their browning), but combine the whole thing at the end just before serving.

6 shelled rock lobster tails, or jumbo prawns (shrimp)
1¼ pounds veal scallops, cut in slices no more than 1 inch wide
Flour for dredging
½ cup butter
1½ pounds mushrooms, washed and sliced
½ cup dry white wine
2 tablespoons chopped parsley
2 tablespoons finely chopped garlic
Juice of 1 lemon
Salt, pepper

No more than 5 minutes before cooking the dish, dredge the lobsters and veal in flour. Shake off any excess flour. Melt the butter in a large skillet. Sauté the lobster quickly, then add the mushrooms and continue cooking until the mushrooms brown lightly. With a slotted spoon, remove the lobster and mushrooms from the pan.

If less than 2 tablespoons of butter is left in the pan, add a bit more and sauté the veal slices quickly, no more than 20 seconds on each side. Add the wine, mushrooms, and lobsters. Ignite the pan with a lighted match, averting your face from the flames. When the flames subside, stir in the parsley, lemon juice, and garlic. Simmer it for 2 or 3 minutes. Serve it with rice.

Makes 6 servings.

SERVING SUGGESTION: Creamed spinach goes nicely. Follow it with a crisp salad or fresh fruit.

WINE: A rich Chardonnay or Sauvignon Blanc.

Cima di Vitello alla Genovese

MODESTO LANZONE

It's worth cajoling, pleading and flattering your butcher to get a big, meaty veal breast to show off this magnificent stuffing of sweetbreads, prosciutto, pistachios, and Parmesan cheese.

The Veal:
   5 pounds veal breast, boned or cut to form a
   pocket

The Stuffing:
   8 eggs
   1 cup (approximately) Parmesan cheese, grated
   1 cup bread crumbs, soaked in milk and squeezed
   dry
   ½ pound sweetbreads, cut into ½-inch cubes
   1 small onion, finely chopped
   ⅓ pound prosciutto, finely chopped or ground
   2 tablespoons olive oil
   1½ teaspoons chopped parsley
   5 ounces fresh pistachios, shelled and chopped

The Braising Liquid:
   1 cup Marsala wine
   3 bay leaves
   2 medium onions, sliced
   1 teaspoon salt
   3 or 4 peppercorns
   2 to 4 cups beef broth, hot

Rinse the veal well, including the cavity. Pat it dry with a paper towel.

In a large bowl, combine the eggs, 1 cup of grated cheese, and the bread crumbs. In a skillet, sauté the sweetbreads, onion, and prosciutto in the olive oil until the sweetbreads are lightly browned and the onion is soft, about 10 minutes on medium heat. Combine the contents of the skillet with the egg mixture, parsley, and pistachios. Use this mixture to stuff the breast. If the mixture seems too loose, add more cheese.

Place the veal breast in a baking pan. Add the remaining ingredients for the braising liquid, using enough broth to cover the veal. Cover the pan with a lid or with aluminum foil. Braise it on top of the stove at a simmer, or in a 325°F. oven for 2 hours. Drain it well before serving.

Makes 12 servings.

SERVING SUGGESTION: For a spectacular meal, precede this with Modesto's Agnolotti (see Index) as a pasta course, and finish with Mama Nina's Crostada di Ricotta (see Index).

WINE: A classic Italian red such as Ghemme or Gattinara, or a nicely aged California Zinfandel or Barbera.

Chinese Kraut and Bratwurst

TRADER VIC'S

I am not a fan of sauerkraut, but after giving it the Trader Vic treatment, I finished every last strand. A long simmer in chicken broth neutralizes the extreme sourness, and a touch of brown sugar adds depth rather than sweetness.

1 large can (1 pound, 11 ounces) sauerkraut
Cold water
1 medium onion, finely chopped
1 medium tomato (ripe), peeled, seeded and
    chopped
2 tablespoons oil
1 tablespoon brown sugar
Salt, freshly ground pepper
1 cup chicken broth
12 bratwurst (veal sausage)
Butter

Drain the kraut, cover it with cold water, and let it soak for 15 minutes. Rinse it well in cold running water.

In a large frying pan, combine the drained kraut, the onion, tomato, and oil. Cook them gently together until the onion is soft, about 10 minutes. Stir in the sugar, about ¼ teaspoon pepper, and the broth. Simmer it uncovered for 25 minutes, or until the liquid just about disappears. Correct the seasoning with salt and pepper.

In another pan, brown the bratwurst in a little butter. Arrange half the sauerkraut in one layer in the bottom of a large baking pan. Arrange the browned bratwurst on top of the kraut and top them off with the rest of the kraut. Bake at 350°F. for 20 minutes.

Makes 6 servings.

SERVING SUGGESTION: Nothing else is needed, except perhaps a loaf of sourdough bread, to make this a perfect peasant meal.

WINE: This process takes most of the tartness out of the sauerkraut, but it still retains something of a tang.

Choose a white wine to serve with it that tends to taste tart without food, such as a Spanish Rioja, a white Graves or a dry Chenin Blanc. Or serve beer.

Roast Pork, Orange Sauce

L'ORANGERIE

L'Orangerie's signature dish is simply a pork roast steamed in foil and served with a brown sauce tinged with orange juice and brandy. It's even delicious the next day sliced and heated through in its sauce.

1 pork rib roast, about 4 pounds
Salt, pepper
1 tablespoon sugar
1 teaspoon vinegar
1 cup fresh orange juice
3 cups veal or chicken broth
1½ cups brown gravy (or, if you have it, demi-glace)

2 tablespoons butter
1 tablespoon brandy
3 oranges
1 tablespoon additional sugar

Heat the oven to 400° F. Season the pork lightly with salt and pepper. Wrap it tightly with aluminum foil. Put it in a baking pan and into the oven for 2 hours.

In a 3- or 4-quart saucepan, cook the sugar with the vinegar until it begins to darken. Add the orange juice and boil it for 10 minutes. Add the broth and continue to boil it until it reduces to 2 cups. Whip the butter, brandy, and brown gravy or demi-glace into the sauce. Keep it warm, but do not let it boil.

Raise the oven temperature to 500°F. (or as high as your oven will go). Unwrap the pork. Brush the roast with the sauce. Quarter 2 of the oranges and place them on top of the pork. Put it in the oven to brown for 10 minutes. Meanwhile, slice the remaining orange for a garnish. When the pork is done, discard the quartered oranges and garnish the roast with the fresh slices. Serve the remaining sauce in a sauceboat.

Makes 6 servings.

SERVING SUGGESTION: Both pork and orange have an affinity for sweet potatoes, which are delicious baked (like a baked potato) in their skins and served plain with a little of the sauce.

WINE: A young, fruity Beaujolais, Zinfandel or Gamay.

Baked Pork with Mojito

SIBONEY

Sour orange and garlic make a magnificent marinade, and a lively sauce for baked pork Cuban style.

The Pork:
2 pounds boneless pork
6 cloves garlic, finely chopped
1 tablespoon dried oregano leaves
1 tablespoon salt
2 sour oranges
Freshly ground pepper
Mojito Sauce (see recipe below)
1 sweet onion, thinly sliced

Cut the pork into chunks of about 1 inch. Place it in a non-aluminum pan or bowl. Add the garlic, oregano, salt, and the juice of the sour oranges. (If you cannot obtain sour, or Seville, oranges, substitute equal parts fresh sweet orange, lime and grapefruit juice.) Let the pork marinate at least 4 hours, or, better, overnight, refrigerated.

Heat the oven to 350°F. Bake the pork in its marinade for about 2 hours, or until it is tender and well done. Serve it with the pan juices or with Mojito Sauce, draped with onion slices.

The Mojito Sauce:
    3 cloves garlic, mashed
    2 tablespoons olive oil
    Juice of 1 sour (Seville) orange

Brown the garlic in the oil. Add the juice of the sour orange, averting your eyes because it will sizzle vigorously. Remove the pan from the heat and pour the sauce quickly over the pork. (This sauce is also delicious on starchy vegetables, such as potato, plantain, yuca or malanga.)

Makes 6 servings.

SERVING SUGGESTION: In Cuban restaurants this is served with black beans and rice and a starchy vegetable such as plantain, yuca, or malanga.

WINE: Italianate reds such as Chianti and Barbera go well with the garlic.

Pork Chop-Apple Casserole

DOIDGE'S KITCHEN

The spicy, sweet sauce that forms in the casserole when the pork chops are done is pure ambrosia.

    6 pork chops, 6 to 8 ounces each, about 1½ inches thick
    18 small white onions (1 pound) peeled
    6 tart apples, cored and quartered
    ½ cup seedless raisins, parboiled until plump, drained
    1 tablespoon brown sugar

1 cup beef broth
Salt, pepper
½ teaspoon grated nutmeg
½ teaspoon ground thyme
½ teaspoon ground mace
¼ teaspoon ground clove
1 tablespoon cornstarch dissolved in 1 tablespoon
  water

Heat the oven to 325°F. Brown the pork chops in a heavy skillet large enough to hold them without overlapping. Arrange the pork chops in a ceramic or earthenware casserole. Scatter the onions, apples, raisins, brown sugar, and broth over the chops, then season it with salt, pepper, nutmeg, thyme, mace, and clove. Feel free to adjust the seasonings to your taste.

Cover the casserole and bake it for 1 hour. Stir in the cornstarch mixture to thicken the juices.

Makes 6 servings.

SERVING SUGGESTION: Accompany the chops with a good fruit chutney.

WINE: A slightly sweet Chenin Blanc, Riesling or Vouvray.

Bacon with Cider Sauce

DOIDGE'S KITCHEN

This is one of those dishes most cooks would flip right past after one glance. A braised slab of bacon? Believe me, you have never had such superb bacon as what you will slice from the bacon "roast." A black chef of my acquaintance says it reminds him of some of the down-home Sunday food he had as a youngster in the South.

1½ pounds slab bacon
1 cup apple cider
4 small peeled onions
2 medium apples, cored and quartered
1½ tablespoons flour
1 tablespoon water
1 tablespoon red currant jelly

Heat the oven to 350° F. Put the bacon in a casserole with the cider and the onions. Bake it covered for 1½ hours. Remove it from the oven, uncover it and add the apples. Turn the bacon over and cover the casserole. Bake it 30 minutes longer.

Put the bacon on a serving dish and slice it like a roast. Surround it with the onions and apples. Pour the cooking juices into a saucepan. Stir the flour, water, and jelly together to make a paste, and stir this into the cooking juices. Bring the sauce to a boil and let it boil for 3 minutes. Pour it over the bacon.

Makes 6 servings.

SERVING SUGGESTION: For a spectacular Sunday brunch, serve this dish with scrambled eggs and English muffins or corn muffins. To let any of the sauce go to waste is criminal.

WINE: No, just coffee.

Carré d'Agneau Assyrien

NARSAI'S

Narsai David's Syrian ancestry suggested the use of pomegranate juice in the marinade for this elegant rack of lamb. It adds a subtle but distinct fruitiness that wine alone does not. Without it, however, the dish is still awfully good.

3 lamb racks
1 cup pomegranate juice, unsweetened
½ cup dry red wine
2 large onions, chopped
3 cloves garlic, finely chopped
1 teaspoon pepper
1 tablespoon basil leaves
1 teaspoon salt

Each rack should have 8 or 9 ribs. If you use the small New Zealand racks, allow 1 whole rack per person. Have the butcher remove the flap meat and chine bone, and French-cut the rib bones. Do not use grenadine instead of pomegranate juice, as this is a sweetened syrup. The unsweetened juice is available in some health food stores. If it is unavailable, increase the red wine by 1 cup.

Purée the juice, wine, onions, garlic, pepper, basil, and salt in a blender or a food processor. Rub this marinade well into the lamb, then pour the remaining marinade over the lamb in a glass or enamel pan. Cover it with plastic wrap and let it marinate in the refrigerator overnight or at room temperature for at least 6 hours.

Heat the oven to 450°F. Wipe off the excess marinade and place the racks of lamb in a roasting pan, fat side down. Roast 10 minutes, then turn the racks up for 10 minutes of roasting for rare, longer for medium or well done. With the small New Zealand racks, decrease the roasting time to 6 to 7 minutes each side.

Makes 6 servings.

SERVING SUGGESTION: Since the dish has no sauce, vegetables such as asparagus or broccoli with hollandaise would be lovely.

WINE: Cabernet Sauvignon or Bordeaux.

Shish Kebab

OMAR KHAYYAM'S

Cubed meat, marinated in something tasty, skewered, and broiled shows up virtually every Middle Eastern cuisine and many European ones. Known variously as shish kebab, shashlik and "en brochette," the only real differences are in the marinating. From San Francisco restaurants, here are three examples, each with its own distinct character. Kebabs are best cooked over a charcoal fire, but the oven broiler can be used effectively.

1 whole leg of lamb (about 5 pounds) or 3 to 3½
    pounds of boneless lamb cut into 1-inch cubes
1 large onion, thinly sliced
1 tablespoon salt
½ teaspoon pepper
⅓ cup dry sherry
2 tablespoons oil
1 teaspoon leaf oregano

If you are using a whole leg of lamb, remove all the fat and gristle, bone it and cut into 1-inch cubes. Or simply use the kebabs cut by the butcher, which are more expensive but more convenient. Combine the lamb with the remaining ingredients in a glass or ceramic bowl. (Or, put everything into a watertight plastic bag and twist it shut with a wire tie.) Let the mixture marinate in the refrigerator overnight, or at least for 3 hours.

Drain the lamb and thread the cubes onto skewers. Broil the lamb to the desired doneness in the oven broiler or, preferably, over charcoal. Serve it with rice pilaf.

Makes 6 servings.

WINE: Cabernet Sauvignon makes a lovely match with simple, grilled lamb.

Boti Kebab

THE TANDOORI

The Lamb:
1 leg of lamb, 4 to 5 pounds
3 or 4 pieces fresh ginger, crushed
3 to 6 cloves garlic, crushed
1 cup plain yogurt
1 teaspoon salt
1 teaspoon pepper
1 teaspoon paprika
1 teaspoon ground cumin
1½ teaspoon ground coriander seed
1 teaspoon lemon juice
2 teaspoons oil
Mint Chutney (see recipe below)

Trim the fat from the lamb. Cut it into 1-inch cubes. Put the crushed ginger and garlic in a small cup. Barely cover it with water. Let this stand for several hours. (This can be done well in advance). Strain the juice. Combine the garlic-ginger juice and the remaining ingredients in a glass or ceramic bowl to make a marinade. Add the lamb cubes and press the marinade into each one with your hands. Cover the bowl with plastic wrap. Let the meat marinate at least 4 to 5 hours, refrigerated if marinated longer.

No skewers in this one. Just spread the lamb on a shallow pan lined with aluminum foil greased with oil. Bake it in a preheated 400°F. oven, turning it as it browns. Serve the lamb when it has browned on all sides, about 15 to 20 minutes. The lamb cubes may also be grilled over charcoal or gas. Serve with Mint Chutney.

Makes 6 servings.

The Mint Chutney:
  1 bunch fresh mint
  1 bunch fresh coriander leaves (cilantro)
  1 teaspoon pepper
  1 tablespoon lemon juice
  1 teaspoon mango powder (see note)
  1 cup plain yogurt
  Salt, to taste

Wash and pick the leaves only of the mint and the coriander. In a blender, purée the leaves, then add the remaining ingredients except salt. Blend for 45 seconds, taste for seasoning, adding salt to taste, and blend again for a few more seconds. Serve as a condiment with spicy foods.

WINE: This is a little sharp for a subtle Cabernet Sauvignon, but a "jug" Cabernet or Ruby Cabernet works well.

NOTE: Chutneys, in Indian cuisine, are condiments, not necessarily the sweet-spicy canned fruit chutneys Americans are most familiar with. The cuisine offers a number of fresh vegetable and herb condiments, such as this one based on mint and cilantro. Mango powder is available in some Oriental food stores. If you can't find it, the sauce suffers little without it. Use the condiment also on fried hors d'oeuvres, such as samosas. It can be made up in advance and frozen in small quantities for up to a year.

Moroccan Lamb Kebabs

AGADIR

1 leg of lamb, about 5 pounds
5 teaspoons ground cumin
4 teaspoons paprika
3 teaspoons white pepper
2 teaspoons black pepper
2 teaspoons turmeric
6 bay leaves
⅓ cup olive oil
2 tablespoons red wine vinegar
2 teaspoons leaf oregano
1 onion, finely chopped
5 cloves garlic, finely chopped
2 to 3 tablespoons butter, melted
Ground cumin

Bone the lamb, trim it of fat, and cut it into ¾-inch cubes. Put the lamb in a glass or ceramic bowl. Add the remaining ingredients, except the butter and additional cumin. Toss the lamb with the seasonings to coat it evenly. Cover the bowl with plastic wrap and let it marinate, refrigerated, for 24 hours.

Thread 4 cubes of lamb on skewers. You should have enough to fill at least 6 skewers. Heat a gas or charcoal grill. Grill the skewered lamb, basting it with the butter every 5 minutes and turning it as it browns. It should be done to medium rare in 10 minutes, depending on how hot the grill is. Just before serving, dust the kebabs lightly with cumin.

Makes 6 servings.

SERVING SUGGESTION: In a Moroccan meal, this is served as an early course, a sort of appetizer. It is not accompanied with vegetables.

WINE: Again, because of the spiciness, a simple red wine, or beer, is preferable to a subtle Cabernet Sauvignon.

Lamb with Honey

AGADIR

Magnificently aromatic, the Moroccan combination of lamb and honey is an inspired one. The ginger gives it a nice bite to offset the sweetness of the honey.

3 pounds boneless lamb shoulder
2 teaspoons white pepper
4 teaspoons turmeric
1 teaspoon powdered ginger
2 teaspoons sweet red (bell) pepper or pimiento, finely chopped
2 teaspoons salt
¾ cup olive oil
¾ cup honey, divided
2 large sweet onions, diced
¾ cup raisins
2 pinches saffron threads, or ½ teaspoon saffron powder
1½ cups blanched almonds

Heat the oven to 350°F.

Cut the lamb into bite-size chunks. Put it in a braising pan, covered skillet or large baking pan. Add the white pepper, turmeric, ginger, sweet red pepper, salt, and all but 1 tablespoon of the olive oil. Stir to coat the lamb with the seasonings and the oil. Put the lamb in the oven. After 15 minutes, check to see that it has browned lightly. If it has not, let it bake uncovered for a few more minutes. When it has browned, add 2 cups of water and ½ cup of the honey. Reduce the heat to 300°F. and cover the pan. Let it braise for 45 minutes to 1½ hours, or until the lamb is tender. The recipe may be done well in advance up to this point, then reheated just before you serve it.

In a skillet, put the remaining olive oil, the onions, raisins, and saffron. Simmer this mixture gently until the onions are soft, about 15 to 25 minutes. Drain the lamb. Put it on a serving plate and top it with the onion mixture (called Mrouzia). Sprinkle the surface with almonds.

Makes 6 servings.

SERVING SUGGESTION: As part of a Moroccan meal, this is a main course. Vegetables are served as appetizers or salads. One eats with one's fingers (right hand only) for proper effect. Therefore, the dish should not be served scalding hot, but given 5 minutes or so to cool slightly.

WINE: A Cabernet Sauvignon, Rosé, or beer.

Lamb Curry

GAYLORD

I must admit I had my suspicions about this recipe when among the ingredients was curry powder. But since the spices cook for so long with the lamb, it turns out to make little difference. The fresh spiciness comes from the garam masala, added at the end to perk things up.

The Lamb Curry:

2 pounds boneless lamb, cut in ¾-inch chunks
2 medium onions, finely chopped or ground, divided
2 tablespoons ground coriander leaves (cilantro)
1 cup plain yogurt
¼ cup oil
2 small pieces fresh ginger, finely chopped or ground
6 cloves garlic, finely chopped
½ teaspoon ground red pepper
1 teaspoon curry powder
2 teaspoons garam masala (see recipe below)
Additional fresh coriander, chopped, for garnish

Marinate the lamb with ½ cup of the onion, the ground coriander leaves, and the yogurt. Marinate it, refrigerated, for at least 4 hours, preferably overnight.

Heat the oil and fry the remaining onions with the ginger and the garlic until the onions are soft and golden brown. Add the red pepper and curry powder and cook for 30 seconds to bring up their aromas. Add the marinated lamb and let it brown on all sides for 5 minutes. Add 1 cup of water, cover the pan and let the lamb simmer until it is tender, about 2½ hours. This may be refrigerated at this point and reheated 20 minutes before serving. Just before serving, stir garam masala into the mixture and garnish the top surface with the coriander leaves.

Makes 6 servings.

The Garam Masala:
   6 cloves
   6 peppercorns
   6 cardamom pods
   1 teaspoon cumin seed
   2 small sticks cinnamon

Combine ingredients and grind them to a fine powder in a blender or a mortar and pestle. Keep any excess ground mixture frozen to ensure freshness.

SERVING SUGGESTION: Plain white rice sops up the tasty liquid.

WINE: Beer is better.

Hot and Sour Lamb

THE HUNAN

A masterpiece of contrasts, this assails the senses with the pungent aromas of vinegar, garlic, and ginger and the sting of red pepper flakes, all of it modified by the wine, the chicken broth, and sesame oil. At The Hunan, the chefs keep a sieve over a small pot so the meat can be drained quickly after the first step and the oil reused from the pot for stir–frying the rest of the dish.

The Lamb:
   ½ pound lean boneless lamb, cut into slices ⅛
      inch thick, ¾ inch wide and 1½ to 2 inches long

The Marinade:
   1 teaspoon cornstarch
   1½ teaspoons Hsao Shing wine or dry sherry
   Pinch of black pepper
   ½ teaspoon vegetable oil

For the Wok:
   2 cups vegetable oil

2 or 3 cloves garlic, finely chopped
2 quarter-size slices fresh ginger, finely chopped
½ cup carrots, cut into 2-inch lengths and sliced thinly lengthwise
½ cup onion, sliced thinly lengthwise
1 teaspoon to 1 tablespoon crushed red pepper
2 tablespoons light soy sauce
Pinch of salt
2 tablespoons chicken broth
2 scallions, including tender green, cut into 1½-inch pieces
1 tablespoon Hsao Shing wine or dry sherry
3 tablespoons vinegar (white, white wine, or cider)
1 tablespoon cornstarch dissolved in 1 tablespoon water
1 teaspoon sesame oil

Mix the lamb with the blended marinade ingredients. Let it marinate for at least 5 to 10 minutes. Heat the oil in a wok over very high heat. (Note that the timings that follow are for the fierce heat of a restaurant stove. On a normal gas stove, double the time.)

Fry the lamb slices in the oil until they are no longer red, about 8 to 10 seconds. Remove the meat immediately and drain off the oil. Remove all but 2 tablespoons oil. Add the garlic, ginger, carrots, and onion. Stir-fry 1 minute. Add the pepper (use the smaller amount first time), soy sauce, salt, and broth. Stir-fry for 15 seconds. Return the lamb to the wok along with the scallions, wine and vinegar. Stir-fry them for 10 seconds. Thicken the sauce with the cornstarch and add the sesame oil. Serve it immediately.

Makes 6 servings.

WINE: Surprisingly, a young, fruity Merlot or St. Émilion stands up well to the strong flavors. Beer is also good, of course.

Lamb Shanks with Yogurt Sauce

CARAVANSARY

Lamb and yogurt have an affinity, a fact most of the Middle Eastern cuisines use to advantage. The yogurt sauce in this example has a definite Lebanese flavor, and a beautiful golden color from the lamb juices.

The Lamb:

6 lamb shanks, about 1 pound each
1 large onion, chopped
4 cloves garlic, chopped
½ teaspoon white pepper
2 teaspoons salt
1 teaspoon dill weed
1 teaspoon basil
2 bay leaves
1 cup chicken broth or water

The Sauce:

4 cups plain yogurt
3 tablespoons flour
3 tablespoons cornstarch
4 egg yolks
1 teaspoon dill weed

Heat the oven to 375°F. Place the lamb shanks in a baking pan large enough to accommodate them without overlapping. Scatter the remaining lamb ingredients over the shanks. Bake them for 2½ hours, turning them every half hour.

Strain the juices from the baking pan and set them aside. Discard all the fat. Add enough water to the juices to make 4 cups. Leave the lamb in the baking pan.

Mix the sauce ingredients in a 3½- or 4-quart saucepan. Slowly bring them to a boil over low heat, stirring with a wire whisk. When the mixture boils, add the reserved lamb baking liquid. Mix it well into the sauce and simmer it to blend the flavors and obtain a smooth texture. Pour the sauce over the lamb shanks and return them to the oven for 30 minutes longer, turning them once.

Makes 6 servings.

SERVING SUGGESTION: A rice pilaf or bulgur pilaf and glazed pearl onions with the lamb.

WINE: St. Émilion or California Merlot.

Lapin aux Pruneaux, Sauce Poivrade

LE RHÔNE

Rabbit is sold in poultry stores and meat markets all over San Francisco, but you seldom see it on a restaurant menu. Le Rhone's marinating process and sharp, peppery sauce give the senses a pleasant jolt. Like many French restaurant recipes, it goes through a seemingly endless number of steps, but the effort is not difficult and the result is delicious.

The Rabbit:
    3 rabbits, each 1½ pounds
    2 or 3 shallots, finely chopped
    2 or 3 sprigs fresh thyme, or ½ teaspoon dried
    4 tablespoons olive oil
    2 bay leaves
    Salt, pepper
    4 tablespoons Cognac (or brandy)

For the Roasting Pan:
    ¼ cup butter

The Prunes:
    15 to 18 prunes
    Zest of 1 orange
    1 tablespoon sugar
    ¾ cup red wine
    Water
    4 tablespoons Cognac or dry sherry

Trim the rabbits. Reserve the trimmings and giblets for the sauce. Split the rabbits between the back legs and the first ribs. Put the rabbits in a glass or ceramic bowl and coat them with the shallots, thyme, olive oil, crumbled bay leaves, salt, pepper, and Cognac or brandy. Cover the bowl with wax paper or plastic wrap and let it marinate overnight in the refrigerator or at room temperature for at least 2 hours. While the rabbit is marinating, plump the prunes by putting them in a bowl with water to cover.

Heat the oven to 350°F. Arrange the drained rabbit pieces in a roasting pan. Dot them with the butter and roast them for 30 minutes, basting them every 5 to 10 minutes. While the rabbit is roasting, combine the drained prunes with the orange zest, sugar, red wine, and water to cover in a saucepan. Simmer them for 30 minutes.

When the rabbit is done, remove the pieces from the pan and discard the cooking butter. Deglaze the pan with the Cognac or sherry over fairly high heat. Remove the pan from the heat and add the drained prunes. Arrange the prunes around the rabbit pieces and spoon on a little of the sauce to decorate the rabbit. Serve the rest on the side.

The Sauce Poivrade:

The trimmings from the rabbits
1 rib celery, diced
1 carrot, diced
1 onion, diced
Butter
1 teaspoon dried thyme, or 3 or 4 sprigs fresh
1 bay leaf
12 peppercorns (approximately), coarsely crushed
½ cup red wine
½ cup red wine vinegar
2 cups brown gravy (or, if you have it, demi-glace)

Sauté the celery, carrot, and onion in a little butter until they are soft. Add the rabbit trimmings and brown them lightly. Add the thyme, bay leaf, and pep- percorns. Cover the pan and let them sweat for 10 minutes to exude their juices. Add the red wine and the vinegar and reduce the liquid to practically nothing. Add the brown gravy or demi-glace and simmer for 1 hour.

Strain the sauce through a sieve. If it is too thick, add some chicken broth or white stock to gain the proper consistency—it should be just thick enough to coat the food.

Makes 6 servings.

WINE: A zippy Côte de Rhône or an assertive Zinfandel.

Vegetables, Cheese & Eggs

Potato Pancakes

SCHROEDER'S

Grated apple is Schroeder's secret ingredient. Come to think of it, we always eat Jewish potato latkes with applesauce, so it makes sense. These are finer-textured than the Jewish version.

3 pounds raw potatoes
4 eggs, lightly beaten
1¼ cups white flour
1½ teaspoons salt
A few grinds of pepper
1 teaspoon grated onion
1 large sour apple, peeled and grated
Lard or shortening for frying

Peel the potatoes and put them immediately into ice water to keep them from discoloring. Shred the potatoes and return them to the ice water. Drain the potatoes. Squeeze them to remove as much moisture as possible. Add the eggs, flour, salt, pepper, onion, and apple.

Heat the lard or shortening in a large, heavy frying pan to a depth of ⅛ inch. Spoon ¼ cup of the batter into the oil, flattening it slightly to form the pancake. Fry 4 or 5 pancakes at a time. Turn them once as they brown on one side. Replenish the fat from time to time.

Drain the pancakes on paper toweling. Keep them warm in the oven but do not cover them. They should be crisp. It is best to serve them immediately.

Makes 6 servings.

Red Cabbage German Style

SCHROEDER'S

No German meal is complete without a little pile of purple strings that turn out to be savory shredded cabbage.

1 whole red cabbage, about 4 pounds
2 cups boiling chicken broth
4 tablespoons butter
2 tablespoons vinegar

2 peeled, diced apples
2 whole cloves
½ cup red wine
1 tablespoon sugar
Salt, pepper to taste
½ stick cinnamon

Peel and discard any wilted leaves from the cabbage. Cut the head in half and remove the core. Shred the cabbage finely and place it in a non-aluminum saucepan holding at least 4 quarts. Pour the broth over the cabbage, add the butter and let it boil for 1 hour.

Add the remaining ingredients and continue cooking the cabbage for 30 minutes longer, stirring it frequently. Taste for seasoning—there should be a balance between sweet and sour so neither dominates.

Makes 6 servings.

Spinach Goma Ae

YAMATO

You wouldn't believe sesame seeds, sugar, and soy sauce could add so much flavor to a vegetable dish. Serve it next to a simple entrée, such as a fried pork chop or roast chicken. The contrast is marvelous.

2 pounds fresh spinach (or 2 packages frozen)
1½ teaspoons toasted sesame seeds
1 tablespoon sugar
2 tablespoons tamari soy sauce

Boil the spinach for 5 minutes in water. Squeeze it dry lightly. Pulverize the sesame seeds in a food processor or in a Japanese suribachi (corrugated grinding bowl). Add the sugar and soy sauce. Mix it with the spinach.

Makes 6 servings.

NOTE: This dish can also be made with horenso (Japanese spinach), shirona (Japanese cabbage), string beans, bean sprouts, or watercress substituted for the spinach.

Victory Garden Dolma

OMAR KHAYYAM'S

In spring and early summer, when the zucchini are growing so fast they balloon to the size of eggplants overnight (well, almost), here is a marvelous way to make use of the big but still tender ones. Start testing the vegetables after 30 minutes. You don't want to get them too soft.

The Vegetables:
  6 large zucchini
  6 small green peppers
  6 medium tomatoes

The Stuffing:
  1 pound ground lamb
  1½ cups cooked rice
  1 onion, chopped (about 1¼ cups)
  ½ cup chopped tomato (use the tops from the 6
    tomatoes, above)
  3 tablespoons chopped parsley
  1½ teaspoons salt
  ¼ teaspoon pepper
  Pinch of chopped mint or tarragon

Heat the oven to 350°F. Cut the zucchini into 3-inch lengths, and hollow each chunk to form cups. Cut the tops off the peppers and remove the seeds. Do the same with the tomatoes.

Mix the stuffing ingredients well. Fill the vegetables with the stuffing. Arrange them in a baking pan. Add 2 cups water to the pan, cover it, and bake it for 45 minutes. Serve the vegetables—1 whole zucchini, 1 pepper, and 1 tomato per serving—moistened with the pan juices.

Makes 6 servings.

Moussaka

XENIOS ZEUS

Recipes for this Greek specialty always look intimidating, with a mile-long list of ingredients and seemingly endless steps. Think of it in these terms and it will seem easy: Layer fried eggplant slices with seasoned ground meat in a casserole and top with a cheese and egg sauce; bake it until the surface browns. That's all there is to it.

The Eggplant:
3 eggplants, cut into ½-inch slices
½ cup olive oil

The Meat:
2 pounds ground meat (lamb or beef or a mixture)
2 tablespoons butter
1 large onion, finely chopped
1 teaspoon salt
3 or 4 grinds of pepper
3 large tomatoes, peeled, seeded, and roughly chopped
3 tablespoons chopped parsley
1 tablespoon leaf oregano
¼ teaspoon nutmeg
¾ cup dry white wine

The Sauce:
3 cups milk
3 tablespoons flour
3 tablespoons butter
1 teaspoon salt
¼ teaspoon nutmeg
3 eggs
3 tablespoons grated Parmesan cheese

For the Casserole:
¾ cup grated Parmesan cheese

Brown the eggplant slices in the olive oil. Set them aside.

In the same skillet, brown the meat in the butter. Add the onion, salt, and pepper to the pan to brown the onion. Add the tomatoes, parsley, oregano, nutmeg, and white wine and let it simmer for 30 minutes.

Scald the milk. In another saucepan, stir the butter and flour together over low heat until they form a smooth mixture. Stir in the milk to make a thin sauce. Season it with salt and nutmeg. Remove it from the heat and beat in the eggs and the cheese. Set it aside.

Heat the oven to 350°F. Grease a 9-by-14-inch baking pan. Spread half the eggplant slices to cover the bottom of the pan, and cover that with half the meat mixture. Spread the remaining eggplant slices over that, then the remaining meat. Pour the sauce over the whole thing and sprinkle it with the grated Parmesan cheese.

Bake the Moussaka until it turns a golden brown on the top surface, 30 to 40 minutes. Boiled cut green beans, rice pilaf or crusty bread are all this needs.

Makes 6 servings.

WINE: A hearty Greek Roditis or a jug red wine.

Ratatouille

DAVOOD'S

Aside from serving as a vegetable side dish, this classic French vegetable stew can be used as an omelet or crêpe filling, as a buffet dish, or a light luncheon dish. It tastes even better reheated. It also freezes well.

The Vegetables:
1 cup olive oil
2 large eggplants, cut in ½-inch cubes
6 zucchini, cut in ½-inch cubes
¾ pound mushrooms, quartered

2 green peppers, seeded and sliced
2 medium onions, sliced

The Sauce Mix:
2 pounds canned plum tomatoes (or fresh, if available)
3 cloves garlic, finely chopped
2 tablespoons honey
1 tablespoon chopped fresh basil (or 1 teaspoon dried)
1 tablespoon chopped fresh oregano (or 1 teaspoon dried)
1½ teaspoons chopped fresh thyme (or ½ teaspoon dried)
1 bay leaf
1 tablespoon salt
1½ teaspoons pepper
1 can (4 ounces) tomato paste

In ⅓ cup of the olive oil, in a large pot or a skillet, sauté the eggplants for 10 minutes. Drain them well and set them aside. Add ½ cup of the oil to the pot and sauté the zucchini and mushrooms until they are barely tender. Drain them well and set them aside with the eggplant. In the remaining oil, sauté the green pepper and onion until they are barely tender. Drain them well and combine them with the other vegetables.

Combine the ingredients for the sauce, mix them well, and add them to the vegetables. Either place the mixture in a large baking pan, cover it with foil, and bake it for 1½ hours at 350°F., or transfer it to a large saucepan or a soup pot and simmer it on top of the stove, stirring occasionally, for 1 to 1½ hours.

Makes 12 generous servings.

Stuffed Tomatoes alla Medici

DOROS

Doros serves this as a side dish to its rich veal dishes, such as the Veal Scaloppine alla Doros (see Index).

6 medium (3 inches in diameter) tomatoes
¼ cup olive oil or clarified butter
1 onion, finely chopped (about ¾ cup)
1 cup (¼ pound) finely chopped mushrooms
Pinch of thyme

1 cup soft bread crumbs
2 teaspoons finely chopped parsley
¼ cup grated Parmesan cheese
2 egg yolks
Salt, pepper
Additional butter or olive oil

Cut the tops off the tomatoes and scoop out the seeds and pulp, leaving shells. Heat the ¼ cup oil in a skillet and sauté the onion in it until it turns golden brown. Add the mushrooms and the thyme. Stir in the bread crumbs and remove the pan from the heat. When the mixture is cool to the touch, stir in the parsley, cheese, yolks, and salt and pepper to taste. Stuff the tomatoes with this mixture.

Butter a baking pan large enough to hold the tomatoes. Put them in the pan and drizzle a bit more butter or oil over the top. Bake them at 375°F. for 25 minutes. Serve them with sautéed or grilled meat.

Makes 6 servings.

NOTE: These tomatoes can be prepared up to a day in advance, then baked just before serving.

Gourmandise de Légumes

ERNIE'S

Layered vegetable mousses have become something of a set piece for devotees of nouvelle cuisine. Actually, the idea is quite old, a forgotten classic. It makes a sort of vegetable parfait. Ernie's serves it with sauce mousseline, a hollandaise with unsweetened whipped cream folded in to lighten it.

The Vegetables:
1 cup purée of white turnips
1 cup purée of broccoli
1 cup purée of carrots
1 cup purée of mushrooms
Salt, pepper

The Custard:
1 cup heavy cream
1 egg
2 egg yolks
Pinch of nutmeg
Juice of ½ lemon

The only vegetables that must be cooked specially for this dish are the mushrooms, which are prepared by puréeing them raw in the food processor or blender, then cooking them dry in a skillet over low heat until they are black. The remaining vegetables can be reserved from occasions when you cook them separately. The approximate amounts necessary to make 1 cup of purée are 2 medium turnips, 1 bunch of broccoli (flowerets only), 2 large or 3 medium carrots, and 1 pound of mushrooms. Season the purées with salt and pepper to taste.

Beat the cream, egg, and yolks together with the nutmeg and the lemon juice just until they are smooth. Add 2 tablespoons of the custard to the turnip purée (or a little more, up to ¼ cup), just enough to make a thick, smooth paste. Repeat the process with the remaining vegetable purées.

Generously butter 6 small (½ cup) soufflé molds or timbales. Fill each one with turnip purée to ¼ its depth. Smooth the surfaces with the back of a spoon and rap them on the table to distribute the purée evenly. Gently top this up to ½ the depth of the container with carrot purée; smooth the surface and rap them on the table. Do the same, up to ¾ of the depth, with the broccoli purée, and finish with the mushroom mixture.

Place the molds in a baking pan, fill the pan to 1 inch with boiling water, and bake them 30 minutes at 325°F. After baking them, let them stand 10 minutes, then invert them onto a plate.

Makes 6 servings.

Swiss Fondue

CALIFORNIA CULINARY ACADEMY

Many of the chef-instructors at the California Culinary Academy are Swiss, so it is not surprising that the national dish of Switzerland shows up on its public menus from time to time. This one is from Chef Sylvio Platl.

1 clove garlic
1½ cups dry white wine
9 ounces Emmenthal cheese, shredded
9 ounces Gruyere cheese, shredded
Salt, white pepper to taste
3 tablespoons cornstarch
⅓ cup Kirsch
2 loaves French bread, cut in ½-inch cubes

Rub a large saucepan or fondue pot with the cut garlic clove. Put the wine in the pot and bring it to a boil. Reduce the heat to a simmer and start adding the cheese, stirring with a wooden spatula. Add it a little at a time so it will melt evenly. Dissolve the cornstarch in the kirsch and stir it into the cheese. Let it cook 2 or 3 minutes, or until it thickens.

Serve the Fondue in a pot over an alcohol burner to keep it warm. Spear a cube of bread with a fork and dip it in the cheese mixture, then eat it. Watch out. The first bite tends to be too hot.

Makes 6 servings.

Joe's Special

ORIGINAL JOE'S

The story goes that a favorite customer of Joe's came in late one night and demanded the chef create him a special dish. All that was left in the larder was some ground beef, cooked spinach and eggs, which the chef threw together. It has become a San Francisco classic. This is not a dish to make for an elegant party, but it is a wonderful way to use up a bit of leftover spinach.

For 1 Very Generous Serving:
½ pound ground beef
½ cup chopped onion
½ pound spinach, cooked in water, drained and
   chopped
1 egg
Salt, pepper

Brown the ground beef with the onion in a skillet, stirring with a fork to break it up into very small pieces. Add the spinach. Stir vigorously to mix it well with the ground beef. This should take about 15 seconds. Break the egg into the pan on top of the beef and spinach. Stir vigorously with the fork to blend it into the mixture as it cooks. As soon as you see no trace of liquid yolk, add salt and pepper to taste and turn the mixture out onto a dinner plate.

VARIATION: Add a handful of sliced mushrooms (about ¾ to 1 cup) to the pan to brown with the ground beef.

Hangtown Fry

SAM'S GRILL

A Northern California classic that dates from the Gold Rush, this concoction was supposed to have been the last-meal request of a convicted murderer just before he was strung up. A more likely story is that a newly wealthy prospector ordered the most expensive dish in a Placerville restaurant (Placerville was known as Hangtown). Since eggs were dear and oysters had to shipped in from the East, both items were horribly expensive. Whatever the start, it has become a classic.

For Each Serving:

2 to 2½ dozen Olympia oysters, shelled
Flour for coating
Egg wash (1 egg beaten with 1 tablespoon milk)
Bread crumbs for coating
Oil for deep-frying or pan-frying
2 tablespoons butter or margarine
2 or 3 eggs
2 slices bacon, browned in their own fat and
   drained

Dredge the oysters in flour. Toss them from hand to hand to rid them of any excess flour, then dip them in egg wash. Finally, roll them in bread crumbs. Deep-fry or pan-fry the oysters for 1 minute. Drain them well and set them aside.

Heat an omelet pan over moderately high flame. Have the butter ready. Beat the eggs with a fork in a small bowl just until they are mixed, about 15 seconds. Put the butter in the frying pan. When the foam subsides, pour in the eggs. Stir them quickly with the flat part of the fork, then, when they have set on the bottom, add the oysters. Don't wait until the top has set —it must still be quite liquid to bind the oysters. Flip the omelet to brown it on the other side. Slip the omelet onto a heated plate and garnish it with the bacon.

SERVING SUGGESTION: If appetite permits, fried potatoes might be appropriate.

WINE: Coffee at breakfast or beer for a late supper.

Beans, Rice & Pasta

Cassoulet

LE CENTRAL

Le Central has kept a pot of beans for its Cassoulet going on the back of its stove continuously since the restaurant opened. That gives us a clue as to how to produce the best Cassoulet—make the beans one day, and serve it reheated the next, with the addition of some fresh meat.

2 pounds dry white beans
5 quarts cold water
3 fresh pork hocks
1 onion studded with 3 cloves
2 or 3 cloves garlic, finely chopped
1½ pounds boneless shoulder of lamb
1½ pounds fresh garlic sausage
1 cup chopped onion
1½ pounds roast pork
1 pound preserved goose (or fresh goose, see note)
1 teaspoon dry mustard
1 teaspoon pepper
1 cup tomato purée

Wash the beans well, then put them in a large pot (at least 8 quarts) with the cold water. Bring them to a boil, let them boil for 2 minutes, then remove them from the heat, cover the pot, and let them soak for 1 hour. Do not drain them.

To the beans, add the pork hock, the onion studded with cloves, and the garlic, re-cover the pot and let it simmer for 2 hours. Drain the juice into another container and reserve it.

Cut the lamb into 1½-inch cubes. Slice the sausage into ¼- to ⅜-inch slices. Brown them together, in the fat rendered from the sausage, in a large skillet. Pour off all but 2 or 3 tablespoons of the accumulated fat in the pan and add the chopped onion. Cook gently until the onion is soft, about 5 to 7 minutes. Add the meat and onion to the beans.

Cut the roast pork into ¼-inch slices and add it to the beans. Brown the preserved goose (or the fresh poultry) in its own fat and add it to the beans. Dissolve the mustard in a couple of teaspoons of cold water and add it to the beans along with the pepper and the tomato purée.

Put the bean mixture into a large casserole or kettle. Add enough of the reserved bean juice to barely cover the beans. At this point, the beans can be set aside or refrigerated until it is time to bake them.

Heat the oven to 375°F. An hour and a half before serving the Cassoulet, put the refrigerated beans into the oven for 30 minutes, uncovered. Then, reduce the heat to 325°F. and continue baking them for 1 hour more. Every 20 minutes or so, break the crust that forms on the surface and baste it with the juices from down in the beans.

Makes 6 servings.

SERVING SUGGESTION: Don't forget some crusty bread. Precede or follow the Cassoulet with a green salad, *et voilà!*

WINE: A hearty red, such as a Côte de Rhône or a California Petite Sirah.

NOTE: Preserved goose is goose meat that is cooked and packed in its own fat. If is available from fancy food stores. As a substitute, use a fresh or frozen goose, the skin removed and the meat pulled from the bones and cut into thick slices. Duck may also be substituted for the goose.

Rice Pilaf

OMAR KHAYYAM'S

Shish kebab is just not the same without it. Come to think of it, no Middle Eastern entrée is the same without rice pilaf. Serve with any broiled or grilled meat.

3 cups long-grain white rice
½ cup butter
6 cups broth (chicken, beef or lamb, or a
　combination)
1½ teaspoons salt
½ teaspoon pepper

Wash the rice well to rid it of its starch. Heat the oven to 400°F.

Melt the butter in a large saucepan. Add the rice and brown it gently and lightly in the butter. Add the broth and the seasonings, cover the pan and put it in the oven. After 30 minutes, remove the pan, give it a stir, cover it again and return it to the oven for 15 minutes.

Serve it with broiled or grilled meat.

Makes 6 servings.

Agnolotti

MODESTO LANZONE

First cousins to tortellini, these come out bigger and with a sort of pasta collar around them, like a cross between tortellini and won tons. Refrigerated, prepared won ton skins, available in San Francisco supermarket produce departments, make a convenient, quick substitute for the dough. The sauce comes out extremely light.

The Filling:
¼ pound raw veal and chicken meat, finely ground
4 tablespoons prosciutto, finely ground or chopped
2 tablespoons finely chopped onion
3 tablespoons butter, melted
½ cup dry white wine
½ teaspoon salt
Dash of pepper
¼ cup grated Parmesan cheese

The Dough:
3½ cups sifted white flour
3 eggs, lightly beaten
1 tablespoon olive oil
1 teaspoon salt
1 egg beaten with 1 teaspoon water

The Sauce:
1 cup heavy cream
2 tablespoons butter
Dash of salt and white pepper
½ teaspoon dry sherry
1 egg yolk

Mix the filling ingredients. Set them aside.

Put the flour in a large bowl. Make a well in the center and add the eggs, the olive oil, and the salt. Knead the mixture until it is smooth, at least 5 minutes, or process it in a food processor. Roll the dough out to a thin sheet, about $1/16$ inch thick. Cut it into 3-inch squares. (If fresh eggroll skins are available, you may use them instead of making the dough.)

Place 1 teaspoon of the filling in the center of a pasta square. Fold it in half, forming a triangle to enclose the filling, and brushing some of the egg beaten with water on the edge to seal the package shut. Curl it into a horseshoe shape.

Bring a large pot containing at least 4 quarts of water to a boil. Add 2 tablespoons salt and the pasta. Boil it for at least 5 minutes, or until the filling is done. Test it by cutting into one. The timing will depend on how generous you were with the filling.

While the pasta is boiling, combine all the sauce ingredients except the egg yolk in a small saucepan. Bring the mixture to a boil, remove it from the heat, and beat in the yolk with a fork to make a light white sauce. When the pasta is done, drain it well, nap it with the sauce and grate on a touch of fresh Parmesan cheese or truffle.

Makes 6 servings, 3 as a main dish.

SERVING SUGGESTION: As a pasta course, follow this with something hearty that doesn't have to be fiddled with much at the last minute, such as the Cima di Vitello (stuffed veal breast) from the same restaurant (see Index).

WINE: A dry Orvieto or French Colombard.

Linguine with Clams in White Sauce

ALIOTO'S

The sauce goes together so fast you don't even start it until the linguine is in the boiling water. It's one of those dishes that are perfect for throwing together at the last minute.

For Each Serving:
  1 tablespoon butter
  1½ teaspoons finely chopped shallots
  2 dozen littleneck clams (shelled and drained) or 1 can (10 ounces) baby clams
  ¼ cup heavy cream
  1½ tablespoons grated Romano cheese
  1 tablespoon chopped parsley
  ¼ pound linguine (thin spaghetti), cooked

Start the linguine in boiling salted water before cooking the sauce. The linguine will probably take longer to boil than it will take to cook the sauce.

Melt the butter in a large skillet. Sauté the shallots in the butter for 1 minute over moderate heat. Add the clams and cook them for 2 minutes. Add the cream and cook for a minute longer. Add the cheese and parsley. When the linguine is cooked, drain it well and stir it into the sauce. When it is totally coated, it is ready to serve.

SERVING SUGGESTION: Like most saucy pasta dishes, this cries out for a crisp green salad to follow.

WINE: A gutsy Chardonnay or Pinot Blanc.

Fettuccine alla Barone

COW HOLLOW INN

A garlicky mushroom sauce laced with Gruyere cheese instead of the usual Parmesan gives this pasta dish made with green (spinach) fettuccine its special character.

For Each Serving:

4 ounces green (spinach) fettuccine
Water
4 tablespoons unsalted butter
1 clove garlic, crushed
3 large mushrooms, thinly sliced
Salt, pepper
¼ cup heavy cream
½ cup shredded Gruyere or Natural Swiss cheese
Grated Parmesan cheese

Boil the fettuccine in salted water until it is al dente (tender but still firm). Drain the pasta in a colander. Cool it under running cold water to stop the cooking.

Melt the butter in a large skillet. Add the garlic and 2 of the mushrooms. Sprinkle them with salt and pepper, and sauté them briefly in the butter. Add the cream, bring it to a boil, and fold in the fettuccine and the Gruyere cheese. When the cheese melts, fold in the remaining sliced mushroom. Serve it immediately, sprinkled with freshly grated Parmesan.

NOTE: This is a large serving; the recipe makes 2 servings as an appetizer.

Potato Gnocchi

FIOR D'ITALIA

The object of the game here is to come out with something reasonably light. That is the reason the potatoes are baked; they should be as dry as possible, so the only moisture comes from the butter and the eggs. I like them with nothing but melted butter and grated cheese, but some prefer an elaborate tomato sauce.

    4 baked potatoes (9 to 10 ounces each)
    2 teaspoons butter
    1 egg yolk
    2¼ cups flour

When the potatoes are cool enough to handle, scoop out the white part. Use the skins for some other purpose. In a large mixing bowl, mash the potato until it has no lumps. Mix in the butter, yolk, and flour to make a light dough. On a lightly floured surface, or between your floured hands, roll the dough into ropes about the thickness of a man's finger, or a breadstick. Cut the rolls into ¾-inch lengths.

Bring a pot of water, to which you have added 1½ teaspoons of salt per quart, to a boil. Cook the Gnocchi in the water until they float to the surface. Try not to put so many Gnocchi in at once that the water stops boiling for a long period. About 2 cups of Gnocchi in 5 quarts of water is right. As the Gnocchi finish cooking, toss them lightly with some melted butter and keep them warm.

Serve the Gnocchi with additional melted butter and grated dry cheese, or with any sauce of your choice, as a first course.

Makes 6 servings.

WINE: Match it to the sauce. A robust sauce demands a robust red wine. Lighter sauces take lighter wines.

Salads

Caesar Salad

GRISON'S

California claims to be the home of this classic American salad, although the evidence seems to indicate it originated in a restaurant in Tijuana, Mexico. It is best made with croutons of stale sourdough bread fried in garlicky olive oil, but any good crouton will suffice.

2 heads romaine lettuce
½ cup olive oil
1 clove garlic
2 eggs
Juice of 1 large lemon
6 to 8 small anchovy fillets
Salt, freshly ground pepper
½ cup grated Parmesan cheese
2 cups croutons

Wash the lettuce well and dry it thoroughly in towels or in a salad dryer. Tear it into bite-size pieces and place them in a large salad bowl. Toss them with the olive oil until the lettuce glistens.

In a smaller bowl, crush the garlic and add to it the eggs (raw or simmered for no more than 1 minute). Squeeze in the lemon juice, and add the anchovies, crushed or cut into tiny pieces. Beat this mixture together and pour it over the lettuce. Toss the lettuce to coat it well, then add salt and lots of freshly ground pepper. Go easy on the salt; the anchovies can be salty enough. Finally, toss in the Parmesan and the croutons.

Makes 6 servings.

Scallops with Lemon Dressing

NOB HILL RESTAURANT, MARK HOPKINS

From nouvelle cuisine comes this warm-and-cold salad of quickly poached scallops over fresh lettuce with a warm vinaigrette. To shred the vegetables, cut them first in long, thin slices, then turn the slices flat and cut them lengthwise into thin filaments. Scattered over the top of the salad, they look quite colorful.

The Dressing:
Juice of 3 lemons
1 tablespoon sherry wine vinegar
¼ cup olive oil
1 teaspoon Dijon-style mustard
Salt, pepper

The Salad:
6 cups broken-up Bibb or butter lettuce, about 3
   or 4 small heads

The Scallops:
1 quart fish stock, or 1 bottle (8 ounces) clam
   juice plus enough water to make 1 quart
3 leeks, white part only, shredded
2 carrots, scraped and shredded
3 dozen scallops, about 2 pounds

Combine the ingredients for the dressing. Beat them with a wire whisk until they form a smooth dressing. Keep this warm in a double boiler.
   Divide the lettuce among 6 salad plates.
   Boil the fish stock with the leeks and carrots for 10 minutes. Drain the vegetables but reserve the stock. Add the scallops and return the liquid to a boil. As soon as it boils, remove the scallops and divide them among the plates. Scatter the shredded vegetables over the surface and ladle on the warm dressing.

Makes 6 servings.

SERVING SUGGESTION: This is designed as a fish course or combination appetizer-salad. Follow it with a light entrée such as Poularde au Champagne (see Index).

WINE: Chenin Blanc or a dry White Riesling.

Salade Marocaine

MARRAKECH

In a multi-course Moroccan meal, in which no eating utensils are used, this is a first course that is eaten according to a special custom. A small piece of bread is held between the thumb and first two fingers of the right hand (never the left). Holding the hand over the salad, fingers pointing down, the bread is held against the thumb while the first two fingers scoop some of the salad against the bread, which is then transported to the mouth. Or you may use a fork.

3 tomatoes
2 green peppers
4 carrots
½ teaspoon ground cumin
3 tablespoons olive oil
1 tablespoon wine vinegar
2 tablespoons chopped parsley

Hold each tomato and green pepper by the stem end with a fork over a high flame until it is charred all over. When the vegetables are cool enough to handle, slip off their skins. Cut them into bite-size chunks. Discard the pepper seeds. Cut the carrots into ½-inch chunks. Boil them until they are just tender, about 15 minutes. Drain them and let them cool.

In a large bowl, beat together the cumin, the olive oil, and the vinegar to make a salad dressing. Toss the vegetables in the dressing and transfer them to a serving plate. Sprinkle them with the chopped parsley. Chill the salad for 30 minutes.

Makes 6 servings.

Artichaut Châtelaine

MAURICE ET CHARLES

California produces all of the commercially grown artichokes in the United States, and Californians consume a substantial percentage of the edible thistle, mostly dipped in drawn butter or mayonnaise. Maurice et Charles lifts the artichoke to the level of the sublime with this salad. Red wine vinegar in the dressing gives it a lovely blush.

The Artichokes:
6 artichokes, peeled down to the heart
2 tablespoons butter
2 teaspoons salt
½ teaspoon pepper
1 lemon, sliced
Water

The Salad:
6 large mushrooms, approximately the same size as the artichoke hearts

The Dressing:
  ½ cup olive oil
  2 tablespoons vinegar or lemon juice
  1 tablespoon Dijon-style mustard
  ½ cup sour cream, lightly whipped
  Salt, pepper
  1 tablespoon fresh dill, chopped (optional)

Put the artichokes in a saucepan with the butter, salt, pepper, and lemon. Add water to cover them, cover the pan with a lid, and boil the artichokes 20 minutes, or until they are cooked through. Test by piercing them with a fork. Drain them. When they are cool enough to handle, scoop out the hairy choke with a teaspoon. Cut them in half lengthwise and let them drain.

Cut the mushrooms in half lengthwise. Alternate artichoke halves and nushroom halves on a salad plate.

With a wire whisk, beat the oil with the vinegar or lemon juice and the mustard. When it forms a creamy sauce, mix in the sour cream, salt and pepper to taste, and the dill. Pour the sauce over the salad.

Makes 6 servings.

OPTIONAL: Serve the salad sprinkled with chopped fresh truffles.

Bay Shrimp in Sour Cream

FOURNOU'S OVENS, STANFORD COURT HOTEL

The addition of horseradish adds a tang and the julienne-cut mushrooms provide unusual texture that lift this salad out of the ordinary.

For Each Serving:
  2 ounces cooked bay shrimp
  3 tablespoons sour cream
  1 teaspoon horseradish
  2 mushrooms, julienne-cut
  ½ teaspoon brandy
  1 lettuce leaf
  ½ teaspoon chopped parsley

In a mixing bowl, combine the shrimp with the sour cream, horseradish, mushrooms, and brandy, tossing them well between each addition. Line a ramekin or salad plate with a lettuce leaf, top it with the salad, and sprinkle the surface with chopped parsley.

Leeks Vinaigrette

LE CENTRAL

Leeks have a special perfume, an aromatic quality that sets them apart from other onions. A simple vinaigrette sets off this characteristic like a picture frame sets off a portrait. The leeks should be quite soft for this recipe, but not so mushy that they lose flavor.

12 leeks, medium size (about 1 inch thick)
4 to 5 quarts of water
¼ cup salt
Vinaigrette sauce (see recipe below)
2 or 3 hard-cooked eggs, finely chopped

Cut off the dark green portion of the leeks, leaving 1 to 2 inches of light green on the stalk. Cut off the hard stem end. Cut an "X" in the light green end about 1 inch deep to facilitate washing the leeks. Rinse them well.

Bring the water and salt to a boil in a pot. Tie the leeks in bunches of 4 with kitchen twine. Boil them for 15 minutes. Drain them and let them cool. Untie the bundles of leeks and arrange them on a serving plate. Pour the sauce over them and sprinkle the chopped eggs on top. This will taste better if it is made up in advance and allowed to marinate for a few hours.

Vinaigrette: Beat 1 teaspoon Dijon-style mustard with 3 tablespoons good wine vinegar, ½ teaspoon salt, and a dash of freshly ground pepper. Slowly beat in ¾ cup vegetable oil (or part olive oil). Taste for seasoning.

Makes 6 servings.

Desserts

Fraises au Champagne

DOMAINE CHANDON

After macerating (soaking) strawberries in Champagne, what is one to do with the strawberry-flavored wine? One answer is to simply pour it back over the strawberries when you serve them, but Chef Janty mixes it in equal parts with crème fraiche to make a light sauce. If you do not have crème fraiche, sour cream tastes almost as good.

3 pints fresh strawberries, rinsed and hulled if
   necessary
1 cup sugar
½ bottle brut champagne
1½ cups crème fraiche or sour cream

Macerate the berries for at least 30 minutes in the sugar and sparkling wine, up to 1 hour if possible. Keep them in the refrigerator during this time.

Drain the berries and divide them among 6 bowls or large goblets. Combine 1½ cups of the macerating liquid with the crème fraiche or sour cream, beating with a wire whisk to make a light, smooth sauce. Pour the sauce over the berries.

Makes 6 servings.

Coeur à la Crème with Strawberry Sauce

GOLDEN EAGLE

The traditional heart-shaped wooden basket mold gives this an engaging appearance, especially surrounded by bright red strawberries. The cream comes out malleable enough to shape any way you like after it drains for a day or so in an ordinary sieve or colander, however.

The Coeur:
1 pound cottage cheese
⅓ pound cream cheese
1 teaspoon salt
1½ teaspoons vanilla extract

¼ cup sugar
1 cup heavy cream

The Sauce:

10 ounces red currant jelly
¼ cup sugar
1 ounce brandy
1 tablespoon lemon juice
2 pints fresh strawberries

With an electric mixer, whip the cottage cheese until it is smooth. Add the cream cheese, salt, vanilla, sugar, and cream and continue whipping until the mixture smooths and stiffens. Line a colander or coeur la crème mold with cheesecloth dampened with water. Transfer the cheese mixture into the cheesecloth-lined mold. Stand the colander over a pan and put the whole thing in the refrigerator to drain for 24 to 36 hours.

To make the sauce, put the jelly, sugar, brandy, and lemon juice in a blender or food processor. Clean and hull the strawberries. Reserve the prettiest strawberries for a garnish and add the rest to the blender or food processor. Process until the mixture is smooth. Keep it chilled.

Unmold the cheese mixture onto a plate. Surround it with the whole strawberries and drizzle a few teaspoons of the sauce over the top. Serve the remaining sauce in a sauceboat. To serve the coeur, cut it into wedges or slices. Serve it with a berry or two and the sauce.

Makes 6 servings.

Strawberry Mousse

RENÉ VERDON'S LE TRIANON

As difficult as it may be to wait until strawberry season is going full bore before making this dish, do it. The riper and redder the strawberries are, the better the mousse will be.

2 cups strawberries, rinsed and hulled
¼ cup sugar
¼ cup dry white wine
1 envelope unflavored gelatin
¼ cup cold water

¼ cup boiling water
1 cup heavy cream, whipped

Set aside the 6 prettiest berries for a garnish. Purée the rest in a blender, food processor or a food mill. Blend the sugar and white wine into the strawberry purée. Sprinkle the gelatin over the cold water to soften it. Stir in the boiling water to dissolve the gelatin. Stir it into the strawberry purée. Fold in the whipped cream. Taste the mixture for sweetness. If the berries are not dead ripe, you may need to add more sugar.

Use individual ring molds or a single 1-quart mold. Divide the mixture among the molds, or pour it into the 1-quart mold. Chill it for at least 3 hours. Unmold the mousse(s) and garnish it (them) with the reserved whole berries.

Makes 6 servings.

WINE: A late-harvest Riesling tastes good with the strawberries and cream cheese.

Cold Soufflé Milanaise

AU RELAIS

The little strips of orange, yellow, and green citrus zest speckle the sea of ivory foam like confetti, which makes colorful a dish that would otherwise be rather pristine. The texture is light, but substantial enough to carry the fresh citrus flavors. Don't let the name soufflé scare you. It's nothing but a Bavarian cream, a kind of mousse.

8 eggs, separated
1 tablespoon sugar
2 tablespoons flour
2 cups milk
2 envelopes unflavored gelatin (2 tablespoons)
1½ cup cold water
4 limes
2 lemons
2 oranges
¾ cup sugar, divided
½ pint heavy cream, whipped

In a mixing bowl, beat the egg yolks with the 1 tablespoon of sugar and the flour. In a medium-size saucepan, bring the milk to a boil. Add about ½ cup of the hot milk to the egg yolks. Stir it well, then beat the yolks back into the hot milk in the saucepan. Heat this custard gently until it thickens, about 2 minutes.

Sprinkle the gelatin into the cold water to soften it. Put it over a pan of hot water to melt the gelatin, then stir it into the custard. Grate the zest (colored portion of the skin) of the citrus fruit into the custard. Squeeze the juices and add the strained juices to the custard.

In a large mixing bowl or a copper bowl, beat the egg whites until they form soft peaks. Add ½ cup of the sugar and continue beating until the meringue forms stiff peaks. Fold the custard mixture into the meringue. Mix the remaining ¼ cup sugar with the whipped cream and fold it into the soufflé mixture.

Butter and sugar a 2-quart soufflé mold. Tie a collar of buttered wax paper around it. Pour in the soufflé mixture right up to the top. Chill the soufflé at least 4 hours.

Makes 6 servings.

WINE: A sweet Gewurztraminer or a light, sweet Muscat goes nicely with the citrus flavors.

NOTE: It is not necessary to make this in a soufflé mold, although it does make a dramatic presentation. It can just as easily be chilled in a large bowl and served as a citrus mousse. If you do use a soufflé mold, remove the collar before serving it.

Cheesecake

DÉLICES DE FRANCE

The definitive French cheesecake. Nothing could be purer or simpler or more heavenly. The citrus peel has the effect of lightening up the richness of the cream cheese and whipped cream.

The Crust Base:
1 cup Graham cracker crumbs
¼ cup butter
1 tablespoon sugar

The Filling:

    12 ounces cream cheese
    ¾ cup sugar
    Zest of 1 lemon, grated
    Zest of 1 orange, grated
    1 tablespoon rum
    Pinch of salt
    1 egg
    1 envelope unflavored gelatin (1 tablespoon)
    2 cups heavy cream, beaten until stiff

Heat the oven to 375°F. Mash the crumbs, butter, and sugar together. Press the mixture evenly into the bottom and part way up the side of an 8-inch springform pan. Bake it for 10 minutes, or until it browns. Let it cool. (Turn off the oven; the cake is not baked).

Beat the cream cheese to soften it, then beat in the sugar, lemon and orange zest, rum, salt, and egg. Sprinkle the gelatin in ¼ cup cold water to soften it. Heat the water gently until the gelatin dissolves, then mix it thoroughly with the cheese. Fold in the whipped cream. Pour and scrape the mixture into the cooled cake pan. Refrigerate it for at least 4 hours.

Makes 10 to 12 servings.

Crostada di Ricotta

MAMA NINA'S

Similar to but lighter than a cheesecake, this filling balances neatly with the cookie-like crust that gives it its name. If the Crostada must be regrigerated overnight, let it warm up to room temperature for about an hour before serving it.

The Crust:

    1½ cups white flour
    ½ cup butter, softened
    2 egg yolks
    2 tablespoons sugar
    1 teaspoon grated lemon zest
    1 tablespoon Marsala wine

The Filling:

    1 pound ricotta cheese
    1 tablespoon flour
    ½ cup sugar
    4 eggs, separated
    1 teaspoon vanilla extract
    ¼ cup sour cream

¼ cup heavy cream
2 tablespoons pine nuts
⅓ cup golden raisins soaked 30 minutes in
   Marsala

Heat the oven to 350°F. Mix the flour and butter until they are well blended. Beat in the egg yolks, sugar, lemon zest, and Marsala. Press half the pastry dough into the bottom of a 9-inch springform pan. Bake it for 8 to 10 minutes. When the pan is cool enough to handle, press the remaining crust onto the sides of the pan. Chill the pan overnight, or at least 4 hours.

Reheat the oven to 350°F. Whip the ricotta. Beat in the flour, sugar, egg yolks, vanilla, sour cream, and heavy cream. Beat the egg whites until they are stiff but not dry. Fold them into the cheese mixture. (If you prefer a denser, richer cake, omit this step. Use the egg whites in another recipe.) Fold in the pine nuts and the raisins. Transfer the mixture to the dough-lined springform pan. Bake the cake for 60 minutes. Let it cool to room temperature, then remove the pan.

Serve at room temperature, but keep it refrigerated if it must stand for longer than a couple of hours.

Makes 8 servings.

Tocino del Cielo

SIBONEY

Literally translated, the name means "heavenly bacon." It dates from the days of the Inquisition, when anti-Semitism ran rampant in Spain and Jews were denied anything good. Those days are long gone, but the name stuck. It's sort of milkless custard. A word of caution: Do not let the sugar syrup cool before mixing it with the yolks, or it will solidify.

1½ cups sugar
¾ cup water
4 or 5 drops of lemon juice
½ cup egg yolks
½ cup whole eggs
1 teaspoon vanilla extract
¼ cup additional sugar

Heat the oven to 350°F. Boil the 1½ cups of sugar with the water and lemon juice until it makes a heavy syrup (225°F.) and it reduces to 1 cup. Beat the egg yolks with the whole eggs. Add the hot syrup and the vanilla and mix it well.

In a heavy skillet, heat the ¼ cup of sugar until it caramelizes. Distribute the caramelized sugar evenly among 6 custard cups or pour it into the bottom of a small baking pan. Tilt the pan to distribute it evenly. Pour the egg mixture through a sieve into the custard cups or the baking pan. Put the custard cups or pan into a larger pan. Pour boiling water around the custard in the larger pan to a depth of at least 1 inch. Cover the cups with foil. Bake the custard until a knife inserted 1 inch from the center comes out clean, about 45 minutes to 1 hour.

Makes 6 servings.

NOTE: It will take approximately 9 egg yolks and 3 whole eggs to make the required amount, but it is better to measure them with a measuring cup.

Granité au Champagne

DOMAINE CHANDON

Technically, a granité is intended to be served between courses to "clear the palate" for what is to come. At Domaine Chandon, the nouvelle cuisine idea of surrounding a simple granité with fresh fruits and berries of the season makes a stunning summer dessert.

½ bottle brut champagne
½ bottle blanc de noir champagne
¼ to ½ cup superfine sugar, to taste
1 teaspoon Kirsch

Mix all the ingredients (using ¼ cup sugar), just enough to blend them and dissolve the sugar. Too much mixing will destroy the lightness contributed by the bubbles in the sparkling wine. Taste the mixture and add more sugar if needed; it should be slightly sweet because it will lose some of its apparent sweetness when it freezes. Pour it into a shallow pan and put it in the freezer. Let it freeze solid.

To serve it, scrape the surface of the ice with a small ice cream scoop to form "snow," which can be scooped up into a ball. Serve it plain between two courses or as a light dessert with fresh berries.

Makes 6 servings.

NOTE: Obviously, Domaine Chandon uses its own sparkling wines to make this dish. However, any good sparkling wine will do the job, using a half-and-half mixture of the driest light champagne you can find and one made entirely of red grape, such as Pinot Noir or Gamay. Some examples are Chandon Blanc de Noir, Schramsberg Blanc de Noir, or Cuvée de Gamay. Do not use pink champagne or cold duck.

Peach Pernod

PHIL LEHR'S STEAKERY

The maitre d' makes a production of sautéing the peach in butter and sugar, finally flaming the whole thing with the anise liqueur. It tastes just as good if you make it in the kitchen and bring the peach and ice cream dessert to the table.

For Each Serving:
1 tablespoon sugar
1 teaspoon butter
¼ lemon
3 tablespoons juice from canned peaches
½ canned peach
1 ounce Pernod (or anise liqueur)
1 scoop vanilla ice cream

In a flambé pan or skillet, melt the sugar and the butter together over low heat. Stir it until the mixture is thick enough to cling to a spoon. Squeeze in the juice from the lemon, then drop the lemon into the sauce. Add the juice from the canned peaches.

Using a fork, spear the lemon and use it to stir the sauce for a few seconds, then remove it. Put the peach and the Pernod into the sauce, turn up the heat, avert your face and ignite the fumes with a match. As the flames die, turn down the heat. Put the peach half on the scoop of ice cream in a dish or a serving cup. Pour the sauce over the peach and serve it immediately.

Délices de Gourmet

MAURICE ET CHARLES

The crème pâtissière serves as a kind of pudding base for fresh fruits of the season in this colorful and dramatic dessert. It's an imaginative variation on the more common fruit tart, only without the crust.

The Sauce:
2 cups milk
Vanilla bean
7 egg yolks
½ cup sugar
½ cup white flour
Few drops orange flower water
½ teaspoon orange liqueur or Kirsch

The Fruit:
4 cups (total) fresh fruit, sliced
¾ cup slivered almonds
2 tablespoons confectioners' sugar

In a saucepan, combine the milk and the vanilla bean. Simmer them together for 10 minutes. While the milk is heating, combine the yolks and the sugar in a mixing bowl. Beat them well until they thicken and "form a ribbon" when poured back into the bowl. (With an electric mixer, this takes about 1½ to 2 minutes.) Beat in the flour.

Remove the vanilla bean from the milk and reserve it for use in another dish. Pour the milk into the egg mixture and mix it well. Return it to the saucepan. Cook, stirring constantly, until it thickens to the consistency of pudding. Remove it from the heat, and stir in the orange flower water and liqueur.

Heat the oven to 400°F. Pour the sauce into a baking pan at least 7½ by 11½ inches. Cover the surface with the sliced fruit. (In spring and summer, strawberries, bananas, peaches, apricots; in fall and winter, apples, pears, bananas, etc.) Sprinkle the surface with the almonds. Bake the fruit for 8 minutes.

Just before serving this dish warm, sprinkle the surface with confectioners' sugar.

Makes 8 to 10 servings.

NOTE: This can be made in any quantity, of course. Adjust the size of the pan and use only as much sauce and fruit as necessary. This sauce will keep in the refrigerator up to a week, in the freezer 6 months.

Soufflé au Grand Marnier

L'ORANGERIE

When your restaurant carries the name of the main flavor of this soufflé, you had better make it well. L'Orangerie makes no deviation from the classic dessert soufflé, a thick pastry cream lightened with egg whites and quickly baked to angelic heights.

2 teaspoons butter, softened
1 cup sugar, divided
2 cups milk
1 tablespoon freshly grated orange zest
6 tablespoons flour
6 eggs, separated
¼ cup Grand Marnier

Heat the oven to 400°F. Use the butter to grease the bottom and sides of a 1½-quart soufflé dish. Sprinkle about ¼ cup of the sugar into the soufflé dish. Tip and shake the dish to spread the sugar evenly, then turn the dish over to knock out the excess sugar.

Combine half the remaining sugar, including the excess from coating the dish, with the milk and the orange zest in a saucepan. Bring it to a boil, stirring to dissolve the sugar. In a mixing bowl, beat the yolks with the remaining sugar and the flour. Add the boiling milk and beat it smooth, then return it to the saucepan. Heat this thick sauce (called crème pâtissière) until it gets very thick. Turn off the heat. (This much can be done in advance and kept refrigerated or frozen.)

Whip the egg whites with a pinch of salt until they form stiff peaks. Stir the Grand Marnier into the crème pâtissière, then fold in the egg whites. Turn the batter into the prepared soufflé dish and bake it for 20 to 25 minutes, or until the top rises 2 inches above the rim of the dish and browns lightly. Sprinkle the top with confectioners' sugar. Serve at once.

Makes 6 servings.

Microwaved Deep-Dish Fruit Pie

THE NUT TREE

The Nut Tree demonstrates how the microwave oven can be used intelligently and with taste. Since a pastry simply warmed in a microwave oven turns to something resembling a rubber toy, the top crust is baked separately to keep it crisp. The microwave oven is perfect, however, for getting the fruit warm without overcooking it, something that happens inevitably when deep-dish pies are baked in a standard oven. The result, something simple and delicious, can only be done with the microwave.

Sugar Mixture:
   2 cups confectioners' sugar
   ½ teaspoon powdered pectin

For Each Serving:
   Pastry lid
   1 cup fresh strawberries, raspberries, apricots, or
      peaches
   ¼ cup sugar mixture (above)

Prepare the sugar mixture by combining the sugar and pectin, and set it aside. It can be kept in a tightly covered container for several weeks.

Make the pastry lids in advance. Use your favorite short pastry recipe (pie crust, pâte sucrée) and roll it out to a thickness of ⅛ inch. Cut the crust into circles exactly the same size as the top of the deep-dish bowls you plan to use for the pies. Bake them on cookie sheets at 400°F. until they are quite brown. Let them cool. These lids can be kept in the refrigerator for several days, or frozen for several months. Note that they shrink slightly when they bake, so they fit inside the bowl neatly.

Prepare the fruit. For strawberries, cut off the crowns and halve them. Leave raspberries whole. Peel apricots or peaches. Cut apricots in half, peaches into thick slices. Put the fruit in a single-serving soufflé dish, a cereal bowl or a deep soup bowl. Gently fold in the sugar mixture and cover the bowl with plastic wrap. Heat the fruit on the high setting in a microwave oven for 1 minute, just long enough to heat it through but not to cook it. The sugar should dissolve and form a kind of a sauce.

Meanwhile, put the pastry lid in a toaster oven or in the broiler for a few seconds to warm through and re-crisp. When the fruit is heated, remove the plastic wrap and lay the lid gently on top of the fruit. Top it with a scoop of vanilla ice cream.

Baked Apple Sundae

THE NUT TREE

The microwave oven makes quick work of forming the juice of the apple, the butter, and the brown sugar into a lovely warm sauce for spooning over ice cream. The apple still has texture and tastes fresh.

For Each Serving:
1 large Rome apple (7 to 10 ounces)
1 tablespoon confectioners' sugar
2 tablespoons brown sugar
Pinch of ground cinnamon
2 teaspoons butter
1 scoop vanilla ice cream

Peel, core and cut the apple in half crosswise. Place the apple cut side up in an individual soufflé dish or a microwave ceramic bowl. Combine the brown sugar and cinnamon and sprinkle the mixture over the apples. Dot the surface with butter, or simply put one pat (1 teaspoon) on each half. Cover the bowl with plastic wrap and keep it refrigerated until time to serve it.

Microwave the apple halves, covered with the plastic wrap, on high setting for 2 minutes each, or until they are cooked through and soft.

Put a hot apple half in a cereal bowl or dessert goblet, top it with a scoop of ice cream and the juices that form in the baking dish.

NOTE: A fresh pear may be substituted for the apple.

Soufflé Carnago

CARNELIAN ROOM

As if a Grand Marnier soufflé, puffed and hot from the oven, were not appealing enough, consider what happens to the flavor when you add banana and chocolate. The chocolate gives the interior of the soufflé a slightly muddy color, but the reward is in the taste.

Butter, sugar for mold
2 cups milk
½ cup sugar
⅓ cup sifted white flour
2 ounces Grand Marnier (or orange brandy liqueur)
1 banana, diced
2 ounces sweet chocolate, diced
5 eggs, separated
2 additional egg whites

Heat the oven to 400°F. Butter and sugar a 6-cup soufflé mold. In a medium-size saucepan, heat the milk and sugar until it comes to a boil. Beat in the flour, stirring with a wire whisk until it thickens creamily. Remove the pan from the fire. Stir in the liqueur, the banana and the chocolate. Beat in the egg yolks.

In a large bowl, beat the egg whites until they form stiff peaks. Fold in the whites, first mixing ¼ of the whites into the sauce to lighten it, then gently folding in the rest of the whites. Transfer the batter to the soufflé mold. Bake it for 20 minutes for a soft center, 25 for a firm center. Serve it immediately.

Makes 6 servings.

The Original Chocolate Decadence

NARSAI'S

Chocolate lovers turn rapturous just thinking about the dense, dark, fudgy cake with its whipped cream icing and raspberry sauce. The last is a touch of genius; the tart raspberries seem to cut through the unctuousness of the devastatingly rich cake.

1 pound dark sweet chocolate
5 ounces unsalted butter (10 tablespoons)
4 whole eggs
1 tablespoon sugar
1 tablespoon flour
1 cup heavy cream, whipped

Shaved bittersweet chocolate
1 package (10 to 12 ounces) frozen raspberries

Flour and butter an 8-inch round cake pan. Cut wax paper to fit the bottom, butter it and lay it on the bottom of the pan. Heat the oven to 425°F.

In a small saucepan over very low heat (or set into a larger saucepan of hot water), melt the chocolate with the butter. Set it aside. In the deep top of a double boiler, combine the eggs with the sugar. Beat the eggs and sugar over the hot water until the sugar dissolves and the mixture is just lukewarm. Remove the top of the double boiler from the heat and beat the eggs until they quadruple in volume and become quite thick.

Fold the flour into the eggs. Stir one-fourth of the egg mixture into the chocolate. Then, fold the chocolate back into the rest of the egg mixture. Pour and scrape the batter into the cake pan. Bake it for 15 minutes. The cake will still be liquid in the center. Freeze the cake overnight in the pan.

To unmold the cake, carefully dip the bottom of the pan in hot water. Invert it onto a cake plate. Remove the pan and gently remove the wax paper. Decorate the cake with whipped cream and shaved bittersweet chocolate. Keep it refrigerated until serving.

Purée the raspberries and their juice in a blender or a food processor. Strain out the seeds, and serve a tablespoon of this purée as a sauce with each portion.

Makes 12 servings.

Walnut-Rum Torte

WARSZAWA

Be lavish when you anoint the split cake with rum-flavor coffee. It should be quite moist. The marzipan filling adds an interesting texture, but if you omit it and simply fill the cake with whipped cream, it's still a spectacular dessert.

The Cake:
10 eggs, separated
1½ cups sugar
1½ teaspoons vanilla extract
1½ teaspoons almond extract
1½ cups finely chopped or ground walnuts
¾ cup Graham cracker meal

¾ cup soda cracker meal
1½ teaspoons baking powder
Pinch of salt

The Coffee-Rum Mixture:
1 cup very strong coffee
2 teaspoons sugar
1 ounce rum

The Marzipan:
1 package (7 or 8 ounces) almond paste
2 or 3 whole eggs

The Whipped Cream:
1 cup heavy cream
1 tablespoon sugar
1 teaspoon vanilla extract

Heat the oven to 375°F. In the bowl of an electric mixer, beat the yolks, the sugar, vanilla and almond extracts for 3 minutes at medium speed. In a separate bowl, beat the egg whites until they are stiff but not dry. Set them aside. Butter an 8-inch springform pan.

Mix together the walnuts, cracker meals, baking powder, and salt. When the yolk mixture is very thick and smooth, blend in the walnut mixture until it is evenly distributed. Fold the beaten egg whites into the yolk mixture, then transfer the batter to the springform pan. Bake the cake for 40 minutes, or until it tests done (a toothpick inserted into it comes out dry).

When the cake has cooled, remove it from the pan and cut it in half into two layers. With a paint brush or a pastry brush, apply the blended coffee mixture generously to the cut sides to saturate the cake. Beat the almond paste with the eggs to make a spreadable marzipan. Evenly spread the marzipan on the cut side of one of the layers, then place the other layer on top.

Whip the cream with the sugar and vanilla until it is stiff. Spread it evenly over the top and sides of the torte. (Optional: Decorate with halved walnuts or sprays of finely chopped walnuts.)

Makes 12 servings.

Date Nut Bread

THE NUT TREE

The Nut Tree is known for its homemade breads, and this dessert or snack loaf is one of the favorites, a fool-proof version of an American classic. It slices beautifully. Spread with cream cheese, it is to die over.

1½ cups diced or sliced dates (about 7½ ounces)
1 teaspoon baking soda
1 cup boiling water
1 cup light brown sugar, firmly packed
2 large eggs, lightly beaten
⅓ cup oil
1 teaspoon vanilla extract
2 cups white flour
1 teaspoon salt
½ teaspoon baking powder
¾ cup coarsely chopped walnuts (3½ ounces)
Brown Sugar Glaze (see recipe below)

Put the dates in a mixing bowl. Combine the soda and the boiling water and pour it over the dates. Let it cool to lukewarm. Meanwhile, heat the oven to 350°F.

Add the brown sugar, eggs, oil, and vanilla, mixing it well with a wooden spoon. Sift the flour with the salt and baking powder. Sift this into the date mixture and beat it with a wooden spoon until it is well mixed, but no more. Fold in the nuts.

Grease 2 medium-size loaf pans (7 by 3 by 2½ inches) or 1 large loaf pan (9 by 5 by 3 inches). Transfer the batter to the loaf pans. Bake the small loaves for 50 to 60 minutes, the large loaf for 65 to 80 minutes, or until a toothpick inserted in the loaf comes out clean. Turn them out on a rack while they are still warm and brush the tops with the Brown Sugar Glaze. Let the breads cool on wire racks. They keep well frozen or refrigerated.

Brown Sugar Glaze: 1 tablespoon each brown sugar, water and corn syrup boiled together for 2 minutes. Apply this while it is still hot.

Makes 1 large or 2 small loaves.

Cream Cheese Apple Pie

VIENNA COFFEE HOUSE, MARK HOPKINS HOTEL

How do you keep the bottom crust of an apple pie crisp without overcooking the filling? You bake the crust and cook the filling separately, and combine them just before topping the whole thing with a cream cheese custard and a sprinkling of crushed cashews.

The Apples:
2 pounds tart apples
½ cup sugar
Pinch of salt
1 tablespoon cornstarch
Pinch of nutmeg
½ teaspoon cinnamon
1½ tablespoons butter
Juice of ½ lemon

The Crust:
Bottom crust for a 9-inch pie

The Topping:
1 pound, 4 ounces cream cheese
½ cup sugar
2 eggs
Pinch of salt
1 teaspoon vanilla extract
¼ cup sliced cashews

Peel, core, halve, and slice the apples. Toss the slices with the sugar, salt, cornstarch, nutmeg, cinnamon, butter, and lemon juice in a large saucepan. Simmer them, uncovered, for 15 minutes, or until they begin to soften and the juice they exude thickens into a sauce. (As a shortcut, simply use a large can of your favorite apple pie filling.)

Heat the oven to 350°F. and bake the pie shell (from a favorite recipe) for 15 minutes. Remove it from the oven and let it cool.

In the bowl of an electric mixer, combine the cream cheese, sugar, eggs, salt, and vanilla extract. Mix it until it is smooth. Fill the partially baked pie shell with the apples. Spoon the cream cheese mixture on top in large splotches, covering the surface. Sprinkle the top with the sliced cashews. Return the pie to the oven for 25 minutes longer. Let it cool, and serve the pie chilled.

Makes 6 to 8 servings.

Pumpkin-Apple Pie

FOUR SEASONS-CLIFT HOTEL

Apples puréed into the pumpkin custard make a fascinating and delicious variation on the standard American pumpkin pie.

The Crust:
1 cup butter
3 eggs
Salt
1 pound (4¼ cups sifted) flour

The Filling:
1 pound fresh pumpkin (or banana squash), peeled and seeded
½ pound (2 medium) apples, peeled, cored and sliced
1 teaspoon powdered cinnamon
1½ cups sugar
¼ teaspoon each orange and lemon zest
½ cup butter
3 cups half-and-half
6 eggs

In a mixing bowl, cream the butter for the crust, then beat in the eggs and salt until it is smooth. Work in the flour, remove the ball of dough from the mixing bowl and let it rest 10 minutes before rolling it out to 1/16 inch. Lay it into 2 pie tins.

Stew the pumpkin, apples, cinnamon, sugar, lemon, and orange zest in the butter for 30 minutes, covered, or until the pumpkin and apples are quite soft. Uncover the pan and let it simmer until the liquid evaporates. Put the mixture into a blender with the cream and eggs. Blend it until it is quite smooth, then pour it into the pie shells. Heat the oven to 450°F.

Bake the pies for 10 minutes, then reduce the heat to 350°F. and bake them for 30 minutes longer, or until a knife inserted an inch from the center comes out clean. If the surface seems to brown too fast, cover it loosely with foil.

Makes 12 servings.

Almond Tart

CHEZ PANISSE

Don't panic if the filling leaks through the cookie crust and makes a bit of a mess. Just cut the tart up as if nothing happened, and watch the ecstatic reaction of anyone who bites into it. This is a good dessert to match with a sweet (late harvest) Riesling.

The Pastry:

1 cup flour
1 tablespoon sugar
½ cup butter
1 tablespoon (or more) water
Few drops almond extract
½ teaspoon vanilla extract

The Filling:

1 cup sliced almonds
¾ cup sugar
¾ cup heavy cream
¼ teaspoon salt
Few drops almond extract
1 teaspoon Grand Marnier

Mix the flour with the sugar in a mixing bowl. Cut in the butter until the mixture resembles meal. Work in the water, almond extract, and vanilla extract to make a paste. Press the paste into a 9-inch tart pan and chill it for 1 hour, or freeze it for future use. Heat the oven to 400°F. and bake the tart for 10 minutes, or until it turns a golden brown.

To make the filling, combine all the ingredients and let them stand until the sugar dissolves, about 20 minutes. Pour the filling into the pre-baked shell, return it to the oven and bake it for 40 minutes, or until the top is brown and the sugar has caramelized. Serve the tart at room temperature.

Makes 6 to 8 servings.

Ice Cream Pie

DOIDGE'S KITCHEN

The chocolate-coconut crust lifts this frozen dessert out of the ordinary. Swirling the three ice creams into a pretty pattern gives it eye appeal.

1 pound semisweet baking chocolate
1 pound shredded coconut
3 pints of ice cream, 3 different flavors

In a heavy saucepan, melt the chocolate over low heat. Stir in the coconut. While the mixture is still warm, press it into a 9-inch pie tin to make a shell. Let it cool.

Scoop the ice cream into the shell, distributing the flavors as best you can, packing the ice cream down to fill the shell to the brim. You probably will not use up all the ice cream. Smooth the surface and put the pie back in the freezer for at least an hour to harden it before serving it.

Makes 6 to 8 servings.

Mud Pie

MACARTHUR PARK

A San Francisco specialty that too few restaurants bother with any more (although it is still quite popular in the private clubs), Mud Pie gets its name from the hot fudge topping that is applied at the last minute. It is important that the fudge be quite hot so it melts the thin layer of fudge already on the pie. Otherwise, it can be too chewy.

The Crust:
6 ounces chocolate cookies
3 tablespoons butter

The Filling:
1½ pints coffee ice cream
1½ pints chocolate ice cream
2 tablespoons espresso coffee
2 ounces Kahlua

The Topping:
2 ounces unsweetened chocolate
1 tablespoon butter

½ cup boiling water
1 cup sugar
2 tablespoons corn syrup
1 teaspoon vanilla extract

Crush the cookies to a fine meal. Mix in the butter to make crumbly paste. Press this evenly into a 9-inch pie pan.

Soften the ice creams and put them in a mixing bowl. Turn on the mixer and beat them on medium speed until they are creamy. Stop the machine. Add the coffee and Kahlua. Turn the machine on again until they are thoroughly mixed in. Transfer the mixture to the pie pan, filling it to the top. Put the pie in the freezer, loosely covered with wax paper.

To make the topping, melt the chocolate in the top of a double boiler over hot water. Add the butter and stir it in until it melts. Stir in the boiling water. Add the sugar and corn syrup and put the pan over direct heat. Bring it to boil and cook it for 6 minutes. Stir in the vanilla and remove it from the heat. It will be quite thick but spreadable. Let it cool slightly, then spread some of it evenly over a 3-inch circle in the middle of the pie. Return it to the freezer. Reserve the remaining fudge.

To serve the pie, first gently reheat the fudge over low heat or in the top of a double boiler over hot water. Cut the pie ino wedges and spoon on a little of the hot fudge.

Makes 6 to 8 servings.

THE RESTAURANTS

AGADIR MOROCCAN RESTAURANT
746 Broadway

Around the corner from the bright lights of North Beach, behind an impressive wrought-iron gate, is a carpeted, plush room exuding typical Moroccan hospitality. It opened in April 1977 and quickly established itself as one of the city's leading Moroccan kitchens. *Lamb with Honey, Moroccan Lamb Kebabs.*

AKASAKA JAPANESE RESTAURANT
466 Bush Street

Two doors from the ornate gate to Chinatown is one of the city's most popular Japanese restaurants. Junji Takemura, who had a successful restaurant by the same name in Tokyo, opened a San Francisco branch in 1974, serving traditional delicacies like the Bento Box, sushi arranged in a lacquered box. *Nasu Dengaka (eggplant appetizer), Steamed Clams.*

ALIOTO'S NUMBER EIGHT
No. 8 Fisherman's Wharf

If the name sounds familiar, it's the same family as the former mayor and the current school superintendent of San Francisco. Founded by Nunzio Alioto in 1928, this has been one of the mainstays of the Wharf. One of the reasons is a magnificent view of the bay and the Golden Gate Bridge. *Marinated Squid, Linguine with Clams in White Sauce, Crab Vinaigrette.*

ASIA GARDEN
772 Pacific Street

The big barn of a dining room, on two floors, is one of the most crowded and popular of the many dim sum restaurants in Chinatown. A Chinese friend refers to it as "Hong Kong style," which means the goodies are wheeled around the room by waitresses who serve them to those who are quickest to point out what they want. It opened in 1972.

Shrimp Bonnet (Har Gow), Su Mi (steamed pork in noodle casing).

AU RELAIS
691 Broadway, Sonoma

Since 1968, when this Victorian house a block from the town square of Sonoma became a French restaurant, it has been ranked among the finest north of San Francisco. It is not unusual to see the chef walk through the outdoor dining area to a row of herbs and snip off a few branches, which are likely to show up on your rack of lamb.

Chicken Gloria, Cold Soufflé Milanaise.

BEETHOVEN
1701 Powell Street

The forbidding countenance of Ludwig himself glowers from the wall, and the stately strains of his music fill the room from hi-fi speakers to provide atmosphere for hearty German fare. So what if Beethoven was really Austrian? The feeling is right in this friendly Washington Square restaurant.

Rindsrouladen (beef rolls).

BLUE FOX
659 Merchant Street

Mario Mondin bought the Blue Fox in 1942 when it was one room and turned it into one of San Francisco's celebrated restaurants. Specializing in Italian and Continental fare, the restaurant possesses one of the more impressive wine cellars in the United States—two of them, in fact. One is used as a private dining room.

Gamberi alla Livornese, Veal Tonne.

LA BOURGOGNE
330 Mason Street

For some San Francisco gourmets, the sun rises and sets over Jean Lapuyade's plush haute cuisine establishment. It has had an impeccable reputation since it opened in 1961, specializing in such dishes as Filet de

Boeuf en Croute, Dover Sole Chambertin, and Soufflé au Grand Marnier.
Sole Chambertin, Duckling with Turnips.

CAFÉ MOZART
708 Bush Street

The handwritten menu changes twice daily, offering different fare for lunch and dinner in this bandbox of a dining room. It's like stepping into a grand family's home in Salzburg, yet you are but a few steps from the Powell Street cable car. It's been open since 1975.
Burgundy Consommé with Escargots, Trout à l' Orange, Chicken in Mustard.

CALIFORNIA CULINARY ACADEMY
205 Fremont Street

A school for chefs, it opened in the summer of 1977 and graduated its first class in the winter of 1979. Shortly after it opened, it began serving luncheons to the public as a means of giving the students practical experience. The menu changes several times a week, providing more of a challenge. Students handle the serving as well.
Trout C.C.A., Coulibiac in Brioche, Swiss Fondue.

CARAVANSARY
2263 Chestnut Street and 310 Sutter Street

Three Middle Easterners of different ethnic backgrounds have developed some striking recipes in these restaurants, attached to cookware-wine-cheese shops. Creativity is the thing, although the Middle Eastern flair is paramount.
Chicken Tabaka, Lamb Shanks with Yogurt Sauce.

CARNELIAN ROOM
Bank of America World Headquarters, 555 California Street

The highest restaurant in San Francisco offers views in all directions from the top floor of the second tallest building in town. (The TransAmerica Pyramid is taller, but it comes to a point and doesn't have a restaurant.) The Carnelian Room is posh and tries to inject California touches into traditional Continental fare.
Poulet Mascotte, Soufflé Carnago.

CASTAGNOLA'S
286 Jefferson Street

The Late Tomaso Castagnola opened the doors on this Fisherman's Wharf mainstay in 1916. Now owned by Andrew Lolli, the restaurant offers a bird's-eye view of the fishermen unloading their catch in the afternoon and early evening. The dining room is actually built out over the bay.

Baked Petrale with White Wine.

LE CENTRAL
453 Bush Street

One block from Chinatown you can step into an atmosphere exactly like that of a Paris bistro, which owners Pierre and Claude Cappelle consciously tried to create when they opened Le Central in 1974. The menu reflects the simplicity—Leeks Vinaigrette, Cassoulet (cooking continuously since the day the place opened), Celery Remoulade and cold Poached Salmon are the high points.

Leeks Vinaigrette, Cassoulet.

CHEZ PANISSE
1512 Shattuck Avenue, Berkeley

Alice Waters, the founder (1971) and current chef, changes the menu daily to reflect whatever she can obtain that is fresh, unusual, and exciting. She maintains a garden that provides most of the vegetables, and she likes to use the charcoal grill for well-marinated meat and fowl. Lindsey Shere is the talented dessert chef who makes a sinful almond tart and magnificent sherbets.

Baked Whole Garlic, Whole Grilled Duck, Almond Tart.

COW HOLLOW INN
2221 Filbert Street

In a beautifully restored Victorian carriage house, the atmosphere is charming and simple. The menu has gone through several transformations with a variety of chefs. The newest, created by Alan Barone, is by far the most creative. Owner Les Dugan aims for a country inn effect.

Cream of Watercress Soup, Fettuccine alla Barone, Stuffed Squab or Cornish Hen with Black Cherry Sauce.

DAVOOD'S RESTAURANT
22 Hiller Avenue, Mill Valley

Practically in the shade of the Muir Woods in rustic Marin County, Davood's serves a menu of Middle Eastern and Continental dishes and a musical mélange of string quartets, woodwind groups, folk music, and soft jazz. The clientele leans toward the vegetarian specialties.

Dolmas (stuffed grape leaves), Ratatouille.

DÉLICES DE FRANCE
320 Mason Street

Jean Lapuyade, owner of the renowned La Bourgogne next door, tried this experiment in 1978, a Parisian delicatessen with freshly made patés and sausages, breads and pastries warm from the oven, and a few tables for dining at lunch. In season, a whole poached salmon is displayed to be cut to order.

Tripe à la Béarnaise, Cheesecake.

DOIDGE'S KITCHEN
3217 Union Street

C. Doidge Baldwin parlayed his sense of adventure in homey food with a taste for what San Franciscans like in refurbished decor into one the more pleasant spots on often-commercial Union Street. Omelets, poached eggs, and hamburgers are the regular specialties, but daily specials and desserts lend an insight into Doidge's own tastes.

Pork Chop-Apple Casserole, Bacon with Cider Sauce, Ice Cream Pie.

DOMAINE CHANDON
California Drive, Yountville

Chandon sparkling wines have quickly risen to the forefront in California. When Moët-Hennessey built its modern Napa Valley facility in 1977, it opened a restaurant with a menu of nouvelle cuisine by a disciple of Paul Bocuse's to show off the wines. It has become so popular, reservations must be made weeks, sometimes months in advance.

Poularde au Champagne, Granité au Champagne, Fraises au Champagne.

DOROS
714 Montgomery Street

One of the mainstays of the Financial District's roster of first-class restaurants, the Northern Italian stronghold specializes in elegance and white-gloved service.

Veal Scaloppine alla Doros, Stuffed Tomatoes alla Medici.

EMPRESS OF CHINA
838 Grant Avenue

Founded in 1968 by a group of San Franciscans, mainly Chinese, who wanted to produce an elegant restaurant in Chinatown, the fifth-floor dining room sports an impressive view, service more like European elegance than Americans expect of Chinese restaurants, and a menu studded with unusual Cantonese dishes like barbecued quail and pressed duck.

Pi Pa Duck, Winter Melon Soup, Dried Scallop Soup.

ERNIE'S
847 Montgomery Street

One of the legendary names of San Francisco restaurants, Ernie's became one of the opulent ones with plush carpets, razzle-dazzle service, a magnificent wine cellar, and sometimes brilliant food. A young chef, Jacky Robert, has introduced some extraordinary nouvelle cuisine dishes.

Gourmandise de Légumes, Chicken with Pears and Endives.

L'ÉTOILE
1075 California Street

A serious French restaurant on Nob Hill, l'Étoile has been producing some of the grandest cuisine for some of San Francisco's grandest folk since 1966.

Mussels "Poulette," Mousse of Duck Liver.

FIOR D'ITALIA
621 Union Street

Once a North Beach jewel, Fior's star faded in the late 1970s until Lee Leardini purchased it in 1978, refurbished it, expanded it, turned the upstairs hotel into a comfortable senior citizens' residence, and generally restored the fading star's glow.

Veal Stelvio, Potato Gnocchi, Chicken Mattone.

FOURNOU'S OVENS
905 California Street (in the Stanford Court Hotel)

The hotel president, Jim Nassikas, comes to his present lofty position from the food and beverage department, and it shows. The love and care lavished on this restaurant is staggering, and the hotel is a favorite with visiting food personalities, among them James Beard.

Cream of Artichoke Soup with Crushed Hazelnuts, Duck with Green Peppercorns and Kumquats, Bay Shrimp in Sour Cream.

FRENCH ROOM (Four Seasons-Clift Hotel)
Geary at Taylor Streets

Better known to locals as the Redwood Room, which is technically the name of the adjoining bar, the dining room of the Clift has always been considered a posh

place for brunch or business lunch and, lately, dinner as well. When the Four Seasons bought it in 1978, the hotel went through an extensive refurbishing, restoring it to its former elegance.
Braised Squabs, Pumpkin-Apple Pie.

GAYLORD INDIA RESTAURANT
Ghirardelli Square

The dining room, on an upper level of the popular shopping and dining complex, overlooks the bay. The kitchen has a bona fide tandoor (clay oven) and chefs imported from India. Part of an international chain, other Gaylords are in London, New York, Hong Kong, and Bombay.
Lamb Curry, Chicken Masala (curry).

GOLDEN EAGLE
160 California Street

Since it opened in 1968, this evocation of old-time San Francisco has been producing some of the most creative food in the city. The Financial District regulars seem to be most appreciative. They keep coming back for more.
Fisherman's Prawns, Chicken San Joaquin, Beef

Vinaigrette, Coeur à la Crème with Strawberry Sauce.

EL GRECO
85 Redhill Avenue, San Anselmo

Marin's pre-eminent Spanish restaurant opened in 1973, closed for most of 1978, and re-emerged as a handsomely redecorated restaurant that could be in Madrid. It is complete with a tapas bar with its own cooking facility, tapas being little hot and cold hors d'oeuvres designed to be eaten with sherry.
Gambas al Ajillo, Fabada Asturiana, Gazpacho Andaluz.

GRISON'S
2100 Van Ness Avenue

A first-class American steak house that still cuts steaks to order and eschews the typical ranch house-steak house decor for a more civilized setting.
Caesar Salad.

THE HUNAN
924 Sansome Street

This is the erstwhile hole-in-the-wall hyperbolized in the *The New Yorker* as "the World's Greatest Chinese

Restaurant." Moved to a former warehouse a few blocks away from its original Chinatown location, The Hunan has grown tenfold in size. Once cramped and friendly in the original building, the new place is rather like a noisy mess hall, but the smoked meats are as fine as ever, and the kitchen remains capable of turning out superb, palate-blistering fare.
Hunan Onion Cake, Hot and Sour Lamb.

INDIA HOUSE
350 Jackson Street

San Francisco's original Indian restaurant, and some say still the best. Opened in 1947 by David Brown, it remains a doggedly authentic North Indian kitchen under the ownership of Sarnan S. Gill.
Murghi Masala (chicken curry).

JACK'S
615 Sacramento Street

California had been a state for only 15 years when Jacques Monique opened a simple little French restaurant in the middle of town. Californians pronounced the name wrong, and the mispronunciation stuck. Through the years, Jack's has been a rock-solid, reliable, and critically acclaimed haven of exceptional food at reasonable prices. It was destroyed during the 1906 earthquake and fire, but rebuilt on the same site exactly as it was.
Chicken Jerusalem.

KAN'S
708 Grant Avenue

One of the venerable stars of Chinatown, Kan's remains a redoubtable kitchen even after the deaths of the founder, Johnny Kan, and more recently his wife, Helen. Founded in 1953, it has always been one of the most successful exponents of Cantonese cuisine, and it's where Danny Kaye perfected his Chinese cooking.
Dry-Fried Prawns in Shell, Almond Chicken.

LITTLE JOE'S
325 Columbus

Until 1978, there were no tables. Everyone sat at the counter and watched owner Frank Montarello operate in front of an eight-burner stove like a symphony conductor. Now there are four tables, whose inhabitants miss the action at the counter.
Cacciucco Livornese.

MACARTHUR PARK
607 Front Street

A modern restaurant with lots of plants and windows looking out on gardens, MacArthur Park follows a strong California theme in its menu and its wines. It is also one of the few restaurants in the city that still serves a classic San Francisco dessert, Mud Pie.

Cucumber and Dill Soup, Lemon Chicken Soup, Mud Pie.

MAMA NINA'S
6779 Washington Street, Yountville

Fresh pasta, fresh vegetables from the garden out back, and lots of food are the hallmarks of this Napa Valley favorite. Many of the winemakers and growers like to eat here because the tone is simple and real.

Crostada di Ricotta.

MAMOUNIA
4411 Balboa Street, (also 200 Merrydale Road, San Rafael)

When a boomlet of Moroccan cuisine hit San Francisco in the 1970's, Mamounia quickly rose to the top of the list, despite its location in the cold reaches of the Richmond District near the ocean.

Harira, Bastilla.

THE MANDARIN
Ghirardelli Square

Cecilia Chiang, the proprietor, is recognized as the doyenne of San Francisco's Chinese cuisine. She holds classes regularly in her restaurant for special groups, which have gone a long way toward dispelling the myths and revealing the truths about Chinese cooking. With its brick walls and exposed wood, the Mandarin is the antithesis of Chinese restaurant decor in the United States—it is modern and luxurious.

Minced Squab, Velvet Chicken.

MARRAKECH
415 O'Farrell

One of the earliest Moroccan restaurants in San Francisco is also one of the most luxurious. No wonder; it is operated by the same people who own l'Orangerie next door, a respected French restaurant.

Salade Marocaine, Lemon Chicken.

MAURICE et CHARLES
901 Lincoln Avenue, San Rafael

Robert Charles is gone (to Santa Rosa), but Maurice Amzallag continues to run a warm, cozy, posh bistro in the heart of Marin County. The menu is dotted with things like truffles and wild boar, and everything is served on fine china and real crystal.

Artichaut Châtelaine, Délices des Gourmets.

LA MÈRE DUQUESNE
101 Shannon Alley

Nouvelle cuisine has made no inroads here; this is old-fashioned country French cuisine, hearty and rich. The mirrored dining room looks bigger than it is, but it is reminiscent of countless Parisian restaurants.

Le Veau de Pêcheur (Fisherman's Veal).

MODESTO LANZONE
Ghirardelli Square

To those who are serious about Northern Italian food, Modesto's is something of a haven. Right across from the Ghirardelli Chocolate Factory, it quietly goes about the business of teaching tourists that spaghetti sauce need not be red and that Italians use herbs other than oregano.

Agnolotti, Cima di Vitello alla Genovese.

NARSAI'S
385 Colusa Avenue, Kensington

Viewers of "Over Easy" on PBS know Narsai David as the one who does the cooking segments. Bay Area food lovers know him as the proprietor of an exciting restaurant dedicated to fresh food and an astounding wine list. The restaurant is modern, done extensively in natural woods. One of the walls is an old water tank.

Mushroom-Clam Velouté, Carré d'Agneau Assyrien, The Original Chocolate Decadence.

NOB HILL RESTAURANT
Mark Hopkins Hotel

In 1978 the Inter-Continental Hotel Group, which owns the Mark, brought in a Parisian chef who installed an extensive nouvelle cuisine menu, one of the first in San Francisco.

Scallops with Lemon Dressing.

THE NUT TREE
Nut Tree, Calif. (near Vacaville)

A favorite stop on Interstate-80 ever since it was a fruit stand under a walnut tree (which still is there—the tree, that is). It has become a complex of restaurants, gift shops, snack bars, and bakeries, but the hub

of it all is the food. The restaurant developed all the dishes itself to epitomize what it calls Western Cuisine.
Pumpkin-Leek Soup, Date Nut Bread, Microwaved Deep-Dish Fruit Pie, Baked Apple Sundae.

OMAR KHAYYAM'S
Powell at O'Farrell

Middle Eastern food was romantic and terribly exotic when George Mardikian opened Omar Khayyam's smack by the end of the Powell Street cable car line in 1938, complete with art nouveau interior and original paintings depicting the *Rubaiyat*. It quickly earned a reputation for serving good food, which it still enjoys.
Shish Kebab, Rice Pilaf, Victory Garden Dolma.

L'ORANGERIE
419 O'Farrell

Roselyne Dupart's intimate French restaurant has been popular since it opened in 1965. She takes its name seriously—the house specialties are pork with orange sauce and Grand Marnier soufflé.
Oeufs Farcis Chimay, Roast Pork, Orange Sauce, Soufflé au Grand Marnier.

ORIGINAL JOE'S
144 Taylor Street

The archetype of a San Francisco genre, an old-fashioned American restaurant with definite Italian contribution. Cooks work in full view of the customers, turning out hamburgers, omelets, scaloppini, fried prawns, and spaghetti rapidly and with flair.
Joe's Special, Braised Oxtails.

PHIL LEHR'S STEAKERY
330 Taylor Street (in the Hilton Tower)

An old-fashioned steak house where one orders one's steak by cut and weight, and back in the kitchen someone actually cuts and trims the meat to order.
Peach Pernod.

PINEBROOK INN
1015 Alameda de las Pulgas, Belmont

A German chef, Klaus Zander, and his wife opened this modern restaurant in a bucolic, garden setting just a few miles south of San Francisco on the Peninsula. The menu leans toward schnitzels and a wonderful roast beef done in salt.
Roast Sirloin in a Salt Coat.

LE RHÔNE
3614 Balboa Street

San Franciscans discover new restaurants worthy of note faster than any other city's population, with the possible exception of New York. Le Rhône was open a week when word started to get around—it's like a French country inn. It's not unusual to find rabbit, pigeon, blood sausage, and unusual desserts on the menu.

Sole Soufflé au Champagne, Lapin aux Pruneaux, Sauce Poivrade.

RITZ OLD POODLE DOG
65 Post Street

A downtown landmark, founded in 1849, and the quintessential old-time San Francisco French restaurant in decor—complete with crystal chandeliers, rose-color Damask, and old crystal glasses.

Chicken à la Ritz.

ROBERT
1701 Octavia

The owner is French but the chef is American, and the menu leans toward the lighter nouvelle cuisine dishes like veal in Champagne sauce. It's in a residential neighborhood in what has come to be known as Baja Pacific Heights, in a lovely old Victorian building.

Cream of Broccoli Soup, Trout Maison.

RUSSIAN RENAISSANCE
5241 Geary Blvd.

A modest, very Russian restaurant, its walls and ceiling covered by big, colorful murals depicting life in medieval Russia, the Renaissance has been quietly going about its business since 1959. One of the popular jewels of the Richmond District.

Hot Borscht, Eggplant Caviar.

SAM'S GRILL
374 Bush Street

Another of the venerable institutions of San Francisco dining, Sam's first opened its doors in 1867. The food is gloriously American, and no excuses. The decor hasn't changed in 100 years.

Hangtown Fry, Chicken Elizabeth, Salmon and Shrimp Newburg.

THE SARDINE FACTORY
701 Cannery Row

A building that was a cafeteria for the workers in a

sardine cannery when John Steinbeck wrote *Cannery Row* now houses one of the more innovative restaurants in California. The walls display historical photos of the fishing and canning era of Monterey, but the menu is strictly up-to-date and lavish.
Sole Vanessi, Veal Cardinal.

SCHROEDER'S
240 Front Street

The daddy of the German restaurants in San Francisco opened in 1893. Aside from its commendable German food, Schroeder's has the distinction of being one of the last restaurants to give up its "men only" rule at lunchtime, which it did in 1970. The original restaurant was destroyed by the 1906 earthquake and fire, and it now stands on its fourth site.
Sauerbraten, Potato Pancakes, Red Cabbage German Style.

SCOTT'S
2400 Lombard Street, and No. 3 Embarcadero Center

In 1976, when it opened, Scott's caused quite a stir; it was a seafood restaurant but there were no hanging nets or stuffed fish on the walls, and it didn't have a salad bar. What it did was serve good, fresh fish, simply cooked. A remarkable success story, by early 1979 Scott's two locations served close to 2,000 meals a day.
Fisherman's Stew, Cioppino.

SIBONEY CUBAN CUISINE
1700 Shattuck Ave., Berkeley

The secret is the motherly Cuban ladies recreating fragrant orange and garlic sauces and yellow rice dishes in the kitchen. Between them and the Cuban drinks from the bar, you could close your eyes and be transported to a Havana bistro of the 1950s.
Baked Pork with Mojito, Arroz con Pollo, Tocino del Cielo.

SPENGER'S FISH GROTTO
19191 Fourth Street, Berkeley

The sprawling expanse of Spenger's dining room filled with happy eaters testifies to the Berkeley mainstay's popularity. The ambitious menu testifies to its reputation for reliable seafood, imaginatively prepared.
Manhattan Chowder, Sole Delmonico.

TAI CHI
2031 Polk Street

This quintessential storefront Chinese restaurant

with only a few tables has a kitchen that turns out food that makes its admirers blissful. Very much a family-style restaurant; no frills, just good food.

Tung-An Chicken, Braised Fish Hunan Style.

THE TANDOORI
2550 Van Ness

What was once a motel coffee shop has been transformed into an authentic North Indian restaurant, complete with imported tandoor (clay ovens), fired by charcoal that turn out succulent chicken and tasty bread. The chefs are also adept at turning out the stew-like dishes non-Indians refer to as "curry."

Boti Kebab, Chicken Shahjahani, Mint Chutney.

TRADER VIC'S
20 Cosmo Place

The flagship of the Trader's worldwide fleet of Polynesian-American restaurants, this is widely considered to be the best. Most of the tourists limit their excursions into Vic Bergeron's wide-ranging menu to the Chinese appetizers, but the kitchen turns out remarkable American and French food as well.

Sweetbreads Trader Vic's Style, Chinese Kraut and Bratwurst.

LE TRIANON
242 O'Farrell Street

René Verdon, who was the White House chef when John F. Kennedy was president, bought the floundering Trianon in 1972 and returned it to its grand Gallic glory. The menu is haute cuisine in the sumptuous style, and the imposing Verdon is capable of producing these dishes masterfully.

Duck with Olives, Strawberry Mousse.

VICTOR'S
St. Francis Hotel, Union Square

One of the first San Francisco restaurants to adopt a largely nouvelle cuisine menu, the rooftop Victor's did it the right way, creating its own dishes instead of slavishly copying the set pieces imported from France.

Oysters Victor, Coupe Madagascar.

VIENNA COFFEE HOUSE
Mark Hopkins Hotel, Nob Hill

Breakfast at the Vienna Coffee House is a kaleidoscope of sweet buns, Danish pastry, and breads. The same bake shop turns out marvelous desserts for lunch and dinner, and the menu leans to sandwiches and soups, as a good coffee shop should.

San Francisco Crab Soup, Cream Cheese Apple Pie.

WARSZAWA

1730 Shattuck Ave., Berkeley

The only Polish restaurant of note in the United States is one of the meccas for Berkeleyites who appreciate homey food served in pleasant surroundings. The wise order one of Nina Pieracka-Girdler's daily specials, something she has concocted from her imagination because she never uses a recipe.

Nalesniki (crêpes), Tort Orzechowy (Walnut-Rum Torte).

WHALING STATION INN

763 Wave Street, Monterey

The heart of the restaurant is an open hearth, where owner John Pisto keeps an oak fire going to broil fresh fish and meat to order. The chef also has a creative touch with seafood sautés.

Hot, Spicy Scallops.

XENIOS ZEUS

2237 Polk Street

A serious Greek restaurant with a menu as deep as the Aegean, Xenios quickly established itself at the forefront of San Francisco's Greek restaurant roster soon after it opened in 1977.

Moussaka.

YAMATO SUKIYAKI

717 California Street

Edward Shigematsu Ishizaki opened Pacific Sukiyaki at Pacific and Powell in 1946, then moved it to its present location in 1950, imported the interior fabricated by Japanese craftsmen in wood and bamboo, and changed the name. It is believed to be the oldest currently operating Japanese restaurant in the United States. Ishizaki's sons—Koichi, Ryozo, and Kenzi—now run the restaurant, one of the prettiest in the city.

Sesame Chicken, Spinach Goma Ae.

INDEX

RESTAURANTS

RECIPES